THIS ISLAND RACE

THIS ISLAND RACE:

Inside 135 years of British bike-racing

Les Woodland

THIS ISLAND RACE:
Inside 135 years of British bike-racing

Copyright © Les Woodland 2005

First published in 2005 by
Mousehold Press
Victoria Cottage
Constitution Opening
Norwich, NR3 4BD
www.mousehold-press.co.uk

Cover design by Terence Loan

ISBN 1 874739 36 6

Printed by Wrightsons, Earls Barton, Northants

CONTENTS

Acknowledgements:
Most of the photographs which appear in this book have been
supplied by courtesy of *Cycling Weekly*. We would like to thank
Cycling Weekly for their kind permission to to reproduce them
here.

Photographic credits:
Author's collection (pp.vii, viii, 24, 78, 89)
Cycling Weekly (pp.37, 40, 45, 99, 105, 119, 132, 139, 144, 171, 175,
188)
Photosport International (p.71)

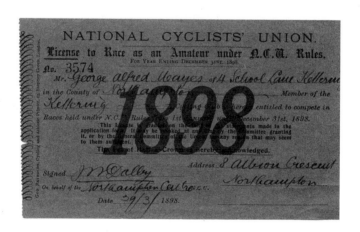

A Licence to race

The boneshaker on which James Moore won the world's first bike race

Parc-de-St-Cloud, Paris, site of the world's first bike race,
from the fountains to the barrier and back, 1868

1

MOORE THE MERRIER

I came across the paint-maker from Rouen so often that in the end he joined in the search. His family as well, although with less good humour. We spent an hour looking for a plaque that I insisted was in the Parc-de-St-Cloud before he gave me one of those straight-faced French looks that hides dry humour and said: 'This isn't a joke like your other one, I suppose?'

'A joke?' I asked, although not with dry humour. Not because I was snooty, but because it hadn't occurred to me it was a joke.

'That an Englishman won the first bike race in the world,' he said. 'Here. In Paris…' He rolled his eyes to heaven in an expression of 'God help me for what I am about to say'… '…in *France.*'

National pride required him not to believe me. It was true, but my case wasn't helped by the fact that the plaque was no longer there. It had gone up on the railings on the centenary of the great race but we couldn't find it. We walked back and forth so much that in the end a man who sold ice cream from a cart with old-fashioned copper lids despaired of our not buying anything and got out his *portable* to call the park's management. There was a lot of *'anglais … commémoratif … première course cycliste … ouais … ouais'* and then a sad look as he told me that James Moore's tribute had been taken down for safe keeping, but that nobody remembered where it was.

The paint-maker from Rouen shrugged and walked off, French pride assaulted but undefeated. His wife and children looked relieved. They didn't share our enthusiasm. The children were more interested in ice cream. Still, at least they'd learned of James Moore, the man who won the first proper bike race in the world. And, dammit, he was British.

I say 'proper' race because there must have been others, of course, kids hurtling round the block, and so on, but this was for all-comers, well advertised and generously provided with prizes. And far from a backstreet tear-up, it was in one of Paris's most glorious parks.

St-Cloud is now a western suburb, just beyond the *périphérique* ring road. The course is still there, a gravelled path between the park fountains and the tunnel under the *périph*. It's worth the trip. Take the *métro* to Pont de Sèvres – don't go to St-Cloud itself because that's further up the hill – cross the river and dodge the traffic and head for a tunnel with the words Parc-de-St-Cloud above it. Stretching away from you will be a wide path to some ornamental fountains 600 metres away. That was where 18-year-old James lined up with the rest of the field. Where you're standing was where they turned before heading back.

These days the park-keeper probably shoos away kids with bikes, but in Moore's time there was such excitement that a crowd turned up in crinolines and top hats and frock-coats. Many carried umbrellas because it had rained that morning and there were still clouds to interrupt the spring sunshine. It was Friday 31 May 1868.

Nobody thought of Moore as English. He came from Bury St Edmunds, in Suffolk, where he lived with his parents in an area called Long Brackland. It's been demolished since then and the best guess is that the family house and workshop – because James Moore senior was a blacksmith and farrier – are now under a supermarket. And nobody knows why they went to France. It was quite a thing in an era when few people had seen a foreigner, still less lived among them. And James and Elizabeth's son was only four.

Nor were the Moores worldly-wise. James senior could write but Elizabeth Ann Moore signed with an X when she registered the birth on 18 January 1849, four days after James's arrival.

The place they moved to in Paris is also no longer there. It was in an alleyway between the Champs-Élysées and the avenue Montaigne, named after one of France's great philosophers, a man who worked out that you didn't have to be well educated to be happy. You'd have to be both well educated and a millionaire to live there now, but in 1854 the streets of central Paris were still full of horses and working men were needed to keep them shod, and their carts repaired.

Little James soon made friends near his new home and they called him *Jimmie Meer*, the nearest they could get to his name. Particularly, he made friends with the Michaux family, which had a woodwork and cart-repair business in the rue Jean-Goujon, at numbers 19–27. You won't find horse-and-cart men there these days. The Christian Dior fashion house has its restaurant there; the Hôtel San Régis across the road costs up to ¤1,000 a night. The site of the Michaux workshops is now occupied by lawyers, but you can look through the tunnel in the modern façade to see the courtyard where Pierre and his sons, Ernest and Pierre, did their work. It was here that some say bicycles first got pedals and really the yard ought to have a plaque of the sort that went up in the park.

Pierre Michaux was a general craftsman, a man variously described as a cabinet-maker, locksmith and carriage-repairer. He was born in 1813, which would put him in his late 40s in May 1861. It was then, so the story goes, that a hat-maker called Brunel, who lived on the other bank of the Seine in the rue de Verneuil, brought his bike to Michaux for repair. 'Bike' is pushing it a bit because it was a heavy monster, a frame of wood and iron suspended between wheels. The front wheel could be steered after a fashion but the only way of moving was to walk, scooting alternately with each leg.

I have no idea what Brunel wanted done but his bike appealed to Ernest, the oldest of the three Michaux sons. He showed it to his brothers Jules and Henri, and their English friend James, and he took it for a scoot through the streets on Sunday morning, when the family didn't work. The ride lasted an hour and he came back weary from pushing the bike uphill, its heavy wheels banging on the cobbles and holes, and from stopping it running away on descents. He could take his feet off the road and let the bike roll but there was little rest because there was nowhere to put his feet.

Next morning, the story goes, his father came up with the idea not only of foot-rests but of levers which would support the legs and put them to work at the same time. Pushing backwards would slow the bike down, pushing them forwards would speed it up. He called his idea the *pédivelle*. Brunel was dubious but the boys were so enthusiastic that he took it along the Champs-Élysées towards the Arc de Triomphe and they ran alongside as he tried to ride.

Of course, for all that Brunel had a *pédivelle*, he had another problem. He had to balance. Until then, nobody had had to. They had their feet on the ground. And he didn't balance well. Sometimes the bike went too fast, sometimes it wouldn't go fast enough, but most of all it wouldn't go straight. The brothers did even worse and sheepishly handed their invention back to its owner, and walked home.

And Moore? Well, he managed it after the same struggles. And others must have succeeded as well because the Michaux family, after a slow start, made more and more of their novel machines. Napoléon III ordered one and the Prince Impérial, Louis-Napoléon, not only rode one but gave a dozen to his aristocratic friends. They rode them through the Tuileries, the gardens at the end of the Champs-Élysées, and the social status of the bicycle was born.

That was why the crowd at the Parc-de-St-Cloud was so well-heeled. It was why René and Aimé Olivier of the Compagnie Parisienne, which financed Michaux's rapid expansion and in 1867 took over the company, put on the race. And it was why the royal family of France, which owned the park, allowed the race there.

The favourite to win was François Drouet and that was the name the crowd shouted as the field of ten set off in billowing dust. He went straight into the lead, followed by a rival named Palocini. But then halfway through the race Moore, the youngest competitor, accelerated 'as fast as lightning' according to *Cycling Record*. He took a lead of twenty metres and won in 3:50 to 'frenetic hurrahs', receiving a gold medal engraved with the image of Napoléon III.

If you want to see it, it's in the city museum at Ely, in Cambridgeshire, along with the winning bike. The machine is a hefty monster with a diamond-shaped iron downtube and a top tube and tyres of flattened metal. The rest is wood, including the wheels. The back wheel is 31 inches across and the front 38, which means the gear was lower for the flat road of the park than Tour de France riders now use to go up mountains.

You couldn't ride a bike like that very fast. It travelled hardly any distance for each turn of the tiny wheels and its speed was limited by how fast the rider could turn his legs. Gearing and the free-wheel had yet to be invented. The challenge, then, became how *far* a rider could go, not how fast. And so, delighted with Moore's success in the race they had sponsored, the Olivier brothers of the Compagnie Parisienne put on a monster event from Paris to Rouen.

The race was promoted through *Le Vélocipède Illustré*, a newspaper which appeared for the first time on 1 April 1869. On 30 September that year the paper announced: 'To further the good cause of the bicycle, it must be determined that the bicycle can be raced over considerable distances with incomparably less fatigue than running. By seeing for itself, the public will be able to appreciate the real merit of the bicycle which makes a maximum economy of time and energy. Therefore we announce to our readers that a first long-distance race will take place in late October. The distance to race will be that separating Paris from Rouen, being a distance of 130 kilometres approximately.' The organiser was Richard Lesclide, personal secretary to Victor Hugo, the poet and novelist who wrote *The Hunchback of Nôtre Dame*. The prizes: 1,000 francs and a bike.

The choice of route may have had something to do with an event in 1868, when two amateurs touring France challenged each other to ride furthest in 24 hours. That was the route they took, from Paris towards Rouen, although they never got there, giving up through tiredness and despair. Somewhere along the way, they were supposed to cross with a group of nine that had set out from Rouen. The nine did get to Paris, though, and in time for dinner.

Moore was quick to enter, noting along with everyone else, the rule that said riders were not 'to be trailed by a dog or use sails'. The paper had said 'late October' but the date was Sunday 7 November, a morning which began with a rainstorm. The start was chaotic. People remembered the excitement of Parc-de-St-Cloud and those who weren't there didn't want to miss out a second time. Crowds were already on the street when riders turned up before dawn to collect their numbers and road maps at the Compagnie Parisienne's offices in the avenue Bugeaud. From there the 325 competitors – the number has been disputed, which shows how chaotic arrangements had become – were expected to ride gently to the Arc de Triomphe for the start at 8 a.m.

Unfortunately there was no concept of cycling clothes and most riders were indistinguishable from the many Parisians who had also bought bikes and decided to join in the procession. The earliest arrivals at the avenue Bugeaud got to the Arc de Triomphe without problem, but the later ones found themselves in a cheering crowd that joined in as they rode along the avenue Victor Hugo. The bigger the bunch, the more excited the onlookers became and the faster the riders and the cycling spectators went in response. Before long they were riding as fast as they could and their thundering iron wheels just made the spectators still more thrilled.

Nobody was sure who was in the race and who not, nor whether it had started. And since they weren't going to take a chance, they thundered past the Arc de Triomphe and down what is now the avenue Charles de Gaulle and off towards Rouen. Pandemonium broke out at the official start, where Moore and the others had been waiting nervously. One of the Olivier brothers expressed 'strong astonishment' at the sight of the fast-disappearing bunch and stewards had to promise the waiting riders they would have 30 minutes deducted from their time in compensation. In fact, there is some confusion over whether the 30-minute delay hadn't already been planned for half the field, to prevent bottlenecks on the road, and whether the 'strong astonishment' wasn't that the first half of the field had abandoned the second, but that it had gone off on a rolling rather than a standing start.

The writer Peter Clifford, who met James Moore's son, reported him in *Sporting Cyclist* as saying that the organisers 'decided to halve the field by a draw of numbers so that evens and odds would leave half an hour apart. A little girl drew from a hat which group would leave first. My father went with the second group, and he was very annoyed. All his rivals were in the first lot, and he declared, "I am an Englishman, after all. I may be the Flying Parisian but you never know what the others might think. It might be a Frenchman they would rather see first."'

So another possibility is that while two groups were intended from the first, their times to be adjusted at the finish, those who actually started first and second may not have been as the promoters intended.

Moore rode on a rare set of wheels with seven 9-mm. ball-bearings. Carts had never needed bearings but bikes had to be moved by a human and not a horse, and the effort produced the need. The invention of ball-bearings is attributed to Jules Suriray, the man in charge of prison workshops. He patented them and set his captive workers to making them. They appeared on the best Olivier bikes and Moore had one.

Riders suffered on the pot-holed roads and the field strung out from the start. A Londoner called J. T. Johnson had dressed in jockey's silks and carried a whip 'to fend off dogs'. He was so exhausted by Vaudreuil at 60 kilometres that he fell off on a railway crossing and couldn't pick himself up. Race officials had to carry him, supported under the arms and legs, to a railwayman's cottage to recover. From there he was taken to be fed at the home of a Monsieur Duval, a local bigwig. Food, as many a bike-rider has discovered since, was all he needed. After an hour of eating and sleeping he got back on his bike, and passed competitor after competitor to finish seventh.

Moore won in front of a huge crowd in a little less than ten and a half hours, reaching the finish in darkness at 6.10 p.m. after 134 kilometres. He'd gone at only twice walking speed but it had been pretty good going. Try riding 134 kilometres down an unsurfaced track without tyres. That'll give you an idea. It certainly surprised the Mayor of Rouen, who was to meet the winners, because he was only just climbing out of his carriage as Moore arrived.

The glory wasn't enough that the organisers saw fit to pay his train fare back to Paris. For that he had to pay 8 francs and 40 centimes – although nothing for the bike because somebody stole it from the café at the finish. It has never been seen again.

The runners-up were the curly haired Count André Castéra, who had come second to Moore at St-Cloud, and a man called Jean Bobillier, from Voiron, on a farmer's bike that weighed 35 kg. Not pounds – kilograms. They came in 15 minutes after Moore and asked to be made equal second. The self-styled Miss America, in reality a hefty British woman who'd been chased by onlookers during the day, finished 22nd at dawn next day, the only woman inside 24 hours. The equally lightly named Miss Olga of Russia didn't finish in time.

As for J. T. Johnson, the 'jockey' who collapsed on the railway lines, he went on to be a star. He set the first World Hour Record, in the series of records which stood until conditions were standardised

7

and a new measure was set by Henri Desgrange. Johnson rode 13 miles 600 yards on the Aston Cross track at Birmingham, a record improved by James Moore at Wolverhampton's Molyneaux Grounds two years later. He rode 14 miles 880 yards.

James Moore went on to become an early World Champion, perhaps the first, when he won the MacGregor Cup that same year. He won again in 1873, 1874 and 1875, and finally in Toulouse in 1877, which is when he retired. Maybe his father told him to stop larking about and make something of his life. Certainly *Jimmie Meer* followed him into the horse trade. He worked at Maisons Lafitte, the Newmarket of French horse-racing, and may well have grown rich enough to own a string of horses himself. He also served in the ambulance corps during the siege of Paris in the Franco–Prussian war in 1870 and 1871, when Parisians were reduced to eating rats and dogs. He was given a French knighthood, becoming a *Chevalier de la Légion d'Honneur*. At some time he moved to 56 Wildwood Road in Hampstead in north London, and there he died on 17 July 1935 after a prostate operation that went wrong.

But a mystery needed to be answered. I knew from Ken Hoxley, formerly a sub-editor on the *Bury Free Press,* that the bike that had won the first race in the world had ended up in the Cambridgeshire village of Witchford. It's one of those linear, yellow-brick villages built along a Fen ridge between fields that would flood if the water weren't continuously pumped into rivers higher than the surrounding land. Hoxley had seen it there, hanging on a garage wall belonging to one of Moore's grandsons. But that had been twenty years earlier. As I knocked at doors and asked in shops it looked as though the trail had gone cold. Then, late in the afternoon, I was directed to a roadside cottage with no door-knocker. It had the air of being abandoned. I banged the woodwork so hard that a neighbour emerged. She told me that an 'elderly gentleman who comes up occasionally from Sussex' wasn't there. She knew nothing of a bike or a cyclist.

More inquiries led to a phone number and eventually a room with shelves of books on the great composers and a newspaper rack with copies of *The Times.* I was in Hatfield, Hertfordshire. My host was Moore's grandson, John Moore, a slightly nervous man as anxious to find out more about his ancestor as I was. And one mystery in particular.

He told me: 'You ask me where he's buried, and I can't tell you. My grandfather died when I was one, but I feel I knew him. My father was a good storyteller but he would never say where my grandfather was buried. It was as if there was some mix-up, something I never understood. There's a family vault in Paris, but I'm sure he's not there. I did hear that he may have been buried somewhere near the Welsh Harp [a reservoir in north London], but I just don't know. It's a mystery.'

The bike that Ken Hoxley saw was the real thing, he said. It was when he left Witchford that he gave the bike to Ely museum, the only place that would take it. Bury St Edmunds had showed no convincing interest in its son and the Science Museum in London wouldn't promise to keep the bike on permanent display. Ely took it because of the local connection and there the bike remains, just to the right of the front door.

At the museum I asked the attendant how many people came to see it. He said there'd certainly been one and he opened the visitors' book. He turned the pages and then, turning it so it faced me, he indicated a name and a signature and said: 'That's him; that's the gentleman who came in.' I recognised the name. It was John Moore, who'd come to see his own grandfather's bike. Hardly anyone else seemed to know it was there. Or not enough, anyway, to mention it to the attendant or write his name in the book.

And the Michaux family? Well, they were never as clever at business as they were with their hands. In 1865 they were making 400 bone-shakers a year. But demand and expansion ran faster than the family could finance. They accepted an investment of 100,000 francs from the Olivier brothers in 1868 and built a factory near the Arc de Triomphe, where 300 workers each made three to five bikes a day. The Oliviers invested another 200,000 francs the following year and by then they owned the company.

The Michaux family claimed it had been unfairly treated but their law case against the brothers failed. They then went into opposition against them, which predictably led the Oliviers to sue the family for breaking its agreement with them. Michaux had to pay 100,000 francs compensation and it ruined him. He died in a pauper's hospital in Paris in 1883.

And the factory? That reached its peak in 1870, with 500 workers and 57 forges. By then, though, apart from rival firms all round the capital, Paris had become besieged by the Germans in the Franco–Prussian war of 1870–71. The Germans pushed back the French advance and surrounded the city. Shells tore through the Parisian air and enough landed on the Oliviers' factory to destroy it.

The final part of the story is that Paris–Rouen ran for a hundred years after Moore won. In 1969 France asked Britain to field a team for the centenary race. That led the British Cycling Federation's racing secretary, Bryan Wotton, to a novel idea. At his home in Rustington in Sussex he told me:

> It occurred to me it would be a lovely idea to field a whole team called Moore. Paris–Rouen wasn't a race where we needed a top-grade team, so I started going through the riders who'd be good enough but wouldn't normally have been selected, but who had the right name.
>
> There was Willi Moore, who was making a name for himself on the track, and a rider in north London called John Moore, and so it went on. It didn't quite work out and we had to make up the numbers with other names but the French really appreciated the idea.

The Pedal Club is a gathering of cycle-trade managers, journalists and other enthusiasts who meet for monthly lunches in London, to mark the history of the sport with their *Golden Book*, and to keep the rumour of cycling alive, and I once asked them to persuade the people who put up blue discs on London houses to place one in Wildwood Road. Ed Taylor, the chairman, lived in Suffolk near Moore's birthplace and said the idea was worth pursuing. But he died shortly afterwards and I doubt anything was done. Certainly there's no plaque, at Wildwood Road or on the supermarket in Bury St Edmunds which stands where Moore was born. Nor on the railings of the Parc-de-St-Cloud. All of which seems a shame.

2

TRACKS OF TEARS

You don't need to employ a French paint-maker to find cycling history closer to home, though. All you have to do is take the London Underground to Islington and walk through a mixture of shabby shops and smart houses to the Business Design Centre. Its role in cycling history is that this is where the first six-day bike race in the world was held.

Originally it was called the Agricultural Hall, and it's where the Smithfield cattle show became established – the first agricultural show at the hall was in December 1862 – attracting as many as 135,000 visitors. It's also where the Cruft's dog show began in 1891, considered a sufficient irritant at the time to provoke an Association for the Suppression of the Dog Show Nuisance in Popular Localities.

There were circuses, too, the first one at Christmas 1863 being described in the local paper as 'on a scale of magnificence hitherto unattempted in this country [with] an immense assemblage of Metropolitan, Provincial and Continental and Colonial artistes of some 350 performers'. Events included steeplechases, military bands and chariot races.

There were further, unbilled excitements: one year a twelve-foot crocodile escaped from its exhibition tank and started off across the hall to the alarm of all within snapping range. Crocodiles can run at 30 mph. In 1864 the lions in an exhibition grabbed an assistant's arm as he poked straw into their cage. The *News of the World* reported that 'it was not until the brutes were nearly blinded with the blows inflicted on their eyes that they were induced to relinquish their grip'.

The front of the building was and remains like a castle, with an arched brick doorway to take horses and carts, and even royal carriages. Behind it is an iron and glass arch like a railway station's. It is so big and enclosed that in 1874 the animals at a farming show there died one by one as one of London's filthy fogs collected under the 123-foot span. The people got out but they left the cows to suffocate. Only the pigs and sheep escaped the cloudy death, and only then because they were nearer the ground and still in relatively untainted air.

The place was going to be pulled down after the second world war, the government having used it for six years as a mail sorting centre and done little to look after it. After that nobody wanted to spend money on it and it rotted. Then in August 1974 the future poet laureate Sir John Betjeman began a campaign to save what, after all, was one of the great Victorian buildings of London. Various plans were proposed and then failed, including an ice rink, a Dickens theme park, and an extension to the Imperial War Museum. Finally, a former Billingsgate fish salesman called Sam Morris bought it in 1984 with money from his family shop-fitting business and he transformed it into the Business Design Centre.

I arranged to go there to meet one of Britain's best amateur and professional riders of the 1970s and 1980s. Mick Bennett – Michael Bennett, these days, now that he's a Man In A Suit – won the Olympic team-pursuit at Montreal in 1976 with Ian Banbury, Ian Hallam and Willi Moore, turned professional, then became a team manager, and finally a race organiser. It was when he worked for the race promotion company run by Alan Rushton that he metamorphosed from Mick into Michael. Of all the Montreal team, he says he was the only one not to be honoured by the Queen.

'It was my penalty for speaking my mind once too often,' he told me. 'I can't say that I think about it every day, but I still feel an unpleasant taste when I do.'

He wasn't 'Michael Bennett' in those days. In fact, the lads called him 'Pretty Boy' for his youthful looks. I don't want to suggest he has gone to seed since then, but the years have given him grey hair and a heavier jaw line. The welcome was as warm as ever, though, and we had a chuckle as we imagined the Queen asking in her little-girl voice: 'Aren't there four in a pursuit team? One hasn't seen the pretty one who made a nuisance of himself, has one?'

I have to add here that when I mentioned the story to Bryan Wotton, who was the British Cycling Federation's racing secretary at the time (and the man who picked all the riders called Moore for Paris–Rouen), he said he couldn't think of anything that Moore had said that would have upset anyone. But that's by the by.

Mick-turned-Michael took me into his glass-fronted office on the edge of the arena, from where he runs the London bike show, and we looked through old ink drawings in his files. Among them were copies of the *Penny Illustrated Paper*. It ran from 1861 to 1913, reporting news from across the Empire. It didn't have photographers in those days and so the illustration of a cyclist on a penny-farthing is an ink drawing. The artist showed him in a long-sleeved buttoned vest, a peaked cap, black mid-thigh shorts, and shoes like slip-ons. His handlebars are curved back and down like a droopy moustache, and he's riding a shallow track edged by posts and canvas. Above him on a suspended cart-wheel are several dozen candles, the best lighting you could get at the time.

What's more interesting than all that though, is that alongside him on an earth trail, is a man on a galloping horse. 'Cowboy v. Cyclist at the Agricultural Hall', said the caption. The date is 19 November 1887. There was no explanation other than to ask the reader to turn to the sports pages, which we didn't have, so we smiled and leafed on through posters of bike shows and other races. And then we found what I'd been looking for: a picture of the world's first six-day race.

It was nine years earlier than the 'Cowboy v. Cyclist' event, in November 1878. The riders had tight trousers with stockings to their knees. Nobody seems to have thought of banking the track to make cornering easier. Nor was there any fencing for either riders or spectators, the penny-farthings riding between rows of well-dressed men in overcoats, only some of whom are shown in the picture as actually watching.

The one link with the modern day was the ornate and iron-fronted balcony sketched into the background. I stood there and gazed down on the arena. Pace out columns and ornate balustrades, and the available area is about 45 by 130 metres. That's tiny for a bike track. In fact there were seven and a half laps to the mile, intensely vertiginous if you were riding it for a week.

The late nineteenth century loved excess and the idea of a six-day bike race came from marathon walks. The first at the

Agricultural Hall was in April 1877 when the American Edward Payson-Weston and Daniel O'Leary of Cork in Ireland (his monument is at Rathbarry, Co. Cork) bet each other £500 they'd be first to cover 500 miles in 135 hours. O'Leary managed it and Weston – who in 1861 walked 453 miles to Abraham Lincoln's inauguration and lost a $10,000 bet through showing up ten hours late – managed 'only' 478 miles. Instead of paying up, they set off again, this time to see who'd drop first. It was Weston, after 510 miles. O'Leary trousered the cash with 520 miles.

There was another race next year. Eighteen of the 23 starters finished, the best of them a man called Conky who had such a lead that he could change his clothes and rest for an hour before starting the last lap. The crowd was impressed but the man from the *Illustrated London News* sniffed that: 'It may be an advantage to know that a man can travel 520 miles in 138 hours, and manage to live through a week with an infinitesimal amount of rest, though we fail to perceive that anyone could possibly be placed in a position where his ability in this respect would be of any use to him [and] what is to be gained by a constant repetition of the fact.'

The crowd would probably also have loved bear-baiting and orphan-stoning. They were in the market for anything that gave them bags of misery and suffering to look at. The promoters guessed, therefore, that if 20,000 people a day would pay to watch walkers, they'd go wild at cyclists, the fastest things on earth and much more likely to endure their miseries publicly. A tired walker, after all, merely sits down; a tired cyclist falls off and possibly brings others crashing down as well. That's much more fun.

For all the pictures in Bennett's files, though, there was no account of the actual race. What had happened? Had it been the body-wrecking, pity-inducing spectacle it's since been painted? It took a three-mile walk to get the answer. And there in a public reference library I found the files of the *Islington Gazette*. The report ran to a lot less than the walking race, but nevertheless it was an account of the first six-day bike race in the world.

Turning the microfiche file, I could read the words in negative on the primitive library screen: 'A bicycle contest was commenced at the Agricultural Hall, on Monday last, for which £150 is offered in prizes for a six days' competition, the money to be allotted thus:-

£100 for the first man, £25 for the second, £15 for the third, and £10 for the fourth.' That was a lot less than for the International Pedestrian Match Championship of the World ('a fair field and no favour, the best man to win; full military band'), which offered the winner £500 and half the gate money.

Only four of the field of twelve were on the track when the race started at 6 a.m. on Monday. The rest joined in when they were ready, seeing it not as a man-to-man battle but a challenge of endurance to be tackled at whatever speed and for however long each day that the riders thought they would survive. Crashes were frequent from the start. The report said:

> At seven o'clock Markham fell heavily, and ten minutes later the Frenchman [Charles Terront, born in St-Ouen in April 1857] came on the track and rattled away in fine style, he at that time being seventeen miles and a half behind the leader, Phillips. The men kept well together for some time after this, but at twenty minutes past nine Markham again came to grief, Andrews falling over him. About half an hour afterwards Phillips and White fell heavily, and in a short time Phillips had to give up all idea of participating further in the contest, his example being followed by Markham after he had completed 78 miles.
>
> Just before five o'clock Stanton took some refreshment whilst riding and in throwing the vessel back to his attendant he swerved slightly, and Evans being close on him a collision occurred, both coming down heavily.

And so it went on, excitement and tedium by turn.

The winner was Bill Cann, billed almost certainly falsely as Long Distance Champion of the North because he came from Sheffield. He led from the start and finished with 1,060 miles. He'd done no training and he lost 7lb. His bike had a 52-inch gear. The firm that made it, Hydes and Wigfull of Whitwell in north-east Derbyshire, was so grateful that it gave him a job.

Like the rest, Cann was wary of Terront. The Frenchman outrageously rode a bike when he wasn't racing, working as a bike-messenger for the Havas picture agency. He openly demanded his prizes in cash. That was too much for British tastes and the home riders thought him appallingly professional, especially the bit about earning money as a messenger. The fact that they, too, were earning money on the track didn't worry them: Terront was a 'typical' Frenchman – bad-tempered, contrary and devious – and that was enough. He hadn't, like the British, won first prize in the lottery of life and could never be expected to be as good.

The more Terront was snubbed, the greater became his contempt for the British and the more the British set out to undo him. The home riders may all have hated each other, Terront said, but they detested him even more and ganged up against him. At one stage the British tried to trick him into a truce and tried to befriend him, he said. They offered him flowers, the French being thought to go in for that sort of thing, and insisted he sniff them. What Terront smelled was a rat; the bouquet had been sprinkled with sleeping powder, he said.

A proper fairy tale would now end with Terront winning the Islington Six, as we'd now call it. I'm afraid he didn't. He won £10, not very professional at all, for coming fifth of the seven who finished the race. He was 160.5 miles behind Cann, many of which he'd lost by having to leave the stadium to find a café when he was hungry while the British riders contrived to have their food brought in to them.

What does finish the tale with a light touch, though, is that Terront learned from that lack of planning when he came to ride a two-man 1,000-kilometre race against Valentin Corre of Brittany in February 1893. The race, on an indoor track in Paris, took 41 hours and 2,500 laps. It was enlivened by two things. The first was that the stadium was so cold at night that the spectators pulled up the seats and made a bonfire. And the second is that Corre, as he put it, was beaten not by the width of a tyre but the length of an inner tube.

The only thing to excite the crowd in what turned out to be a terribly tedious race was that both men seemed to ride for 27 hours without a pee. When Corre finally cracked and ran to his cabin with the world's most painful bladder, his rival continued to lap the track serenely. Reports say Corre lost six laps every time he stopped.

Next morning a paper revealed the trick – *Le coup de la chambre à air,* the headline gloated. A *chambre à air* is an inner tube. What reporters had seen, but Corre hadn't, was that Terront had handed one of his pacers a length of inner tube with a knot tied in one end. Come the moment, all he had to do was call his helpers around him as he rode, stuff the inner tube up the inside of his shorts and then hand the finished job to a helper to empty. That's no mean trick on a free-wheel; on a fixed-wheel it's close to a circus act. The revelation brought new interest to the race and crowds queued down the block. Prices at the ticket office doubled and so many packed into the stadium, sitting on the rafters, standing ten-deep on the fragile balconies, that the police had to be called to restore safety.

Terront finished the 1,000 kilometres in 41:50:4, with Corre 9.3 kilometres behind. Spectators carried Terront in triumph. Corre, meanwhile, could see the joke. 'Terront didn't beat me by a tyre,' he said. 'He won by an inner tube.'

And one last thing. Think of Terront if ever you ride Paris–Brest–Paris. He was its very first winner, in the days when the race really did seem, in the words of the organiser, to go 'to the end of the world and back'.

3

TRIALS OF OUR TIMES

For a woman with such a role in the story of British bike-racing, it's odd that her name has vanished. All we know is that on 21 July 1894 she was travelling gently along the North Road about 60 miles outside London when she got tangled up in a bike race. What happened next was to affect cycling history for half a century.

To understand what happened, we have to wind the film back. You see, if James Moore had returned to Britain after Paris–Rouen, he'd have found none of the road-races he could have ridden in France. Or, rather, he'd have found something rather different.

Bikes didn't take off as quickly in Britain. Moore won his pioneering race in May 1868, but it was only that year that the first *vélocipèdes* reached England. A man called Rowley Turner saw young blades riding them in the streets of Paris, bought one for himself and took it to the Coventry Sewing Machine Company. His uncle, who owned the firm, started making copies and for a while made a healthy living.

The following February, Turner set off to ride the 53 miles from London to Brighton, accompanied by two other cyclists – 19-year-old John Mayall ('son of the well-known photographer') and Charles Spencer – and a reporter from *The Times* in a coach drawn by two horses. It took them fifteen hours and in the following months two members of the London Stock Exchange walked it faster. But *The Times* was so impressed that it headlined an 'EXTRAORDINARY VELOCIPEDE FEAT'.

> They had a preliminary run round Trafalgar Square and started off at a rate of eight miles an hour … against a strong head wind all the way. They kept pretty close together as far as Crawley (30 miles) after which Mr Mayall took a decided lead

and arrived in Brighton, and his two friends shortly after, all in good condition for dinner and the second part of a concert at the Grand Hall.

That seemed great fun to lads all over the country and they started 31 cycling clubs within eight years. They must have raced, of course, if only between themselves. And because there are always people who like organisation and structure, four clubs – the London, Surrey, Temple and Pickwick – got together in November 1877 to form the Bicycle Union. They drank it into formal existence the following February at the Guildhall Tavern in Gresham Street in London.

This may not have been cycling as we know it. The winner of the Bicycle Union's first 25-mile championship at Stamford Bridge was the Hon. Ion Keith-Falconer, a man so detached from life outside Cambridge University that he told his mother in 1881 that cycling 'keeps young fellows out of the public houses, music halls, gambling Hells and all other traps'. A bike race, he reported, was 'as quiet and respectable as a public science lecture'. That could be a young lad doing a bit of wool-pulling over his mother's eyes. But that wasn't the Hon. Ion's style. A serious chap, Britain's first cycling champion: he went on to become professor of Arabic at Cambridge, an authority on shorthand, and a missionary.

Having toffs in the sport didn't help with the authorities, though. Cyclists were unpopular for their rumbling wheels and bugle calls, and the way they lounged around in villages they visited, crowding noisily into post offices to send telegrams to prove how far they'd ridden. 'The captain often carried a bugle which he blew to signal "mount", "dismount" or "slacken speed",' says the writer Ray Hallett in *Cycling On*. 'The riders … carried whistles, bells or pneumatic horns called *cyclornes* to warn people of their approach. This was necessary because in the days before the motor car, people almost always walked in the middle of the road, and on warm summer days dogs liked to sleep in peaceful village streets.'

In other words, people warmed to cyclists in the way they now welcome being hooted out of the way by a speeding driver. And, as Ray Hallett continues: 'Practical jokes were rougher then than they are now and village lads with nothing much to do on their days off work sometimes amused themselves by ambushing cyclists in some quiet lane. Dogs were set at the riders or sticks pushed through the wheels. Even worse, a thin wire might be stretched across the road between two trees causing a frightful crash.'

Then there were stagecoach drivers who realised that a world with bikes would be a world that didn't need coaches. In the spirit of suppressing the opposition, the driver of the St Albans mail coach in Hertfordshire, Henry Cracknell, carried a contraption of ropes and weights he could swing at cyclists unhappy enough to come within range. In 1876 he felled the entire Trafalgar Bicycle Club, for which he was fined £5.

Until then, of course, horses had been the fastest things on the road. Except for other animals and pedestrians, they were the *only* things on the road. It wasn't just the sheer speed of cyclists that upset people; it was their sudden, silent arrival, their seemingly wayward behaviour in a previously ordered life, and the way they regarded the road as their own. When Cracknell whirled his bolas and brought the Trafalgar Club to its Waterloo, there were many who sympathised more with him and his £5 fine than they did with his victims.

In the summer of 1878 the law came close to forcing cyclists off the road altogether. A change to the Highways Act would have made cycling illegal. Denied the pleasure of a ban through the campaigning of the Bicycle Union themselves, the police took to harassing 'road-scorchers' instead. Even a gentleman of 'a most respectable address' was fined 40 shillings in 1882 for riding through London at a 'furious' 10 miles per hour, reported *The Cyclist.*

In the countryside, though, informal races had turned into formal ones and then into established challenges which attracted riders from the limited area in which they could travel in those days. One of the first promoters of formalised races was the North Road Club, named after the principle road from London towards Scotland. Its aims, when it began in 1885, were 'to promote fast and long-distance cycling on the Great North and other roads'.

Things moved so quickly that in January 1895 the *Rational Dress Society Gazette* enthused that 'the North Road really has become a cycling track as well as a thoroughfare for all non-cyclists'. (The Rational Dress Society, by the way, will turn up again later; its main interest, which sounds bizarre now, was to promote the right of women to wear bloomers.) And that was the trouble. People didn't actually want their roads turned into race-tracks, even though the magazine's report may have been a cheerful exaggeration of the situation. They didn't want panting men racing furiously and unannounced along roads which until then had seen nothing more dramatic than the occasional coach, or herd of driven cows.

Things grew worse when 'scorchers' copied their colleagues on the track and raced with 'escorts' to 'bring them along', as reports put it. Pacers, in other words. The result was mass charges for the line twice as big as they had previously been. That was just more than the police would tolerate. 'Often horse-mounted policemen charged at racers and threw sticks into their wheels,' says one report.

In September 1893 the magazine *Cycling* printed cartoons by P. E. Kemp which showed continental racing as a paradise where soldiers protected cyclists as they raced down the centre of the road – and then depicted a British mounted policeman chasing one rider while two more bend over another who, we're to assume, had been brought down by a truncheon through the spokes. 'Hounded by the police', says Kemp's caption.

And that's how our anonymous lady comes into the story. On 21 July, 1894 she became tangled up with some of the 50 riders, many with pacers, in a 50-mile race on the North Road. The field had split into small groups and one, including riders called Freddie Bidlake and Arthur Ilsley, was just passing the woman and her horse when it panicked and reared, and pushed them into a ditch. The *Cycling* journalist Dennis Donovan, writing of that era a century later, said: 'Bidlake went under the horse, but [other riders] had the presence of mind to get to the horse's head and steady him before Bidlake suffered any further injury.'

No great damage was done to anybody, although the bikes were ruined and the woman's tranquillity rattled. She complained to the Chief Constable of Huntingdonshire, saying she thought things of this nature had been stopped, and the police said that from now on they would be. The National Cyclists' Union – the renamed Bicycle

Union – had already urged organisers to switch their races to tracks and many of the big events had made that move. Now, a fresh assault on the image and, potentially, the rights of cyclists in general meant that it took fright that any more racing would bring another attempt to ban all cycling: it forbade all racing on the road.

'The National Cyclists Union as a public body desires to discourage road-racing … and prohibits any of its officials from officiating or assisting at any road-races and refuses to recognise any records made on the road', it resolved at its annual meeting in 1888.

Well, you can't forbid things without people taking exception. It was a lesson that the NCU never learned. It was all very well saying there'd be racing on tracks, but most people didn't live near tracks. They lived near roads, and when they tried to outdo each other, it was on roads that they did it. The first move was to create a breakaway body, the Road Records Committee, almost immediately renamed the Road Records Association. It simply adopted the NCU's records as its own and invited anyone who cared to try to break them. And there were more road-races, too, like the one that upset the woman on the horse.

By now, even the rebels could see they were pushing their luck. They needed a fresh approach. They wouldn't race on the track, or couldn't because they didn't have one near them, and now they couldn't charge about in bunches. Something new was needed, and it came from the North Road Club on 5 October 1895. It ran not a road-race but a time-trial. They didn't tell officialdom they were going to do it, and if the police happened to inquire, well, it couldn't be a race because all the riders were alone. How could you have a race in which competitors often never saw each other?

Les Bowerman, who researched the history of these new races against invisible rivals, says: 'What distinguished this from earlier unpaced races was that the riders started at intervals of "two or three" minutes in reverse handicap order, the fastest first. Company riding was not forbidden but was unlikely to occur. This would then be very similar to a time-trial as we know it.'

The NCU was frustrated beyond description. It was a dignified association of well-meaning officials who wanted no more than to keep the roads open to cyclists in an era when that was by no means guaranteed. And, yet, whatever they did, those same cyclists refused to be saved, or some of them, anyway. In some ways the rebels must have felt like tribesmen confronted by their first interfering missionary. The underlying message was wise, but it was depressingly sensible. The jungle had worked perfectly well before the missionary came and, while some sought to take the new path, the rest just got on with things as they had been in the days when fun hadn't become a sin.

What was so aggravating about the NCU is that it was so nit-picking. It saw cycling as a sport for gentlemen, which is why it found it so easy to fall in line with the police. It had, too, a high-minded persistence that no racing-cyclist should receive a prize in cash, nor receive any prize that could be of use in cycling. That was to preserve that gentlemanly aspect by keeping the sport determinedly pure and amateur. It did little to endear itself to working-class men from whom cycling took their very last penny.

Gentlemen make rotten street-brawlers, though, and the NCU went into a long sulk as the rebels became not only successful but larger than the NCU itself. It lost interest and involved itself almost entirely with track-racing. Its sulk lasted until 1921, when it finally recognised that time-trialling had come to stay and gave it its blessing.

Meanwhile the rebel movement became established. Its opening meeting, involving eleven clubs, was called by 'Biddy' Bidlake, the North Road man whose cropper in his own club's event had made the whole thing necessary.

Bidlake was already an influential man, at least in his own region. He is often credited with being the father of time-trialling, but it'd be better to call him the father of formalised time-trialling. There had, after all, been races of different sorts for many years, including some against the clock, but there is no doubt he was the sport's first really influential thinker.

The time-trialling writer Bernard Thompson, in *Alpaca to Skinsuit*, says he 'shaped and structured the sport … [his] greatness resulted from his deep love of the sport. At one time he was the holder of the 50, 100-mile, 12 and 24-hour tricycle records on both road and track.'

In 1933 the magazine *Cycling* created a *Golden Book of Cycling* to honour the sport's leading benefactors and performers, and that year 7,000 cyclists watched Bidlake sign the first page at a concert in the Albert Hall in London. It was the last time most of them saw him. He was riding down Barnet Hill in north London a few weeks later when he crashed with a car and died. The sport scattered his ashes on his beloved North Road at Girtford Bridge, 48 miles from London and 148 miles from York, and built him a memorial garden there. His memorial stands beside another, to George Herbert Stancer, who comes into our story later.

F. T. Bidlake – the father of organised time-trialling and British cycle sport's first major influence

Time-trialling became the biggest part of racing in Britain. The emergency stopgap had become *the* sport. But Bidlake and the NCU had begun an isolation from the rest of world cycling that would last for 50 years. The NCU favoured track-racing, but the tracks were crumbling and the grandstands emptying; the rebel RRA became the Road Time Trials Council, the biggest racing body in the country. You'd think this would bring self-confidence. Far from it. The police weren't stupid – they knew what was going on – but the RRA (later known as the RTTC) nevertheless maintained a fiction of secrecy. Races were at dawn and deep in the countryside. Lists of riders were headed 'Private and confidential'. Even *Cycling* was asked not to print the dates, venues or start-times of races, a ban with which it co-operated. Such limited publicity as existed spoke of a race on a course coded as F4 or E72. Dates were given only as 'weekend 12' or 'weekend 20'. Riders carried not only no numbers (although by contrast they had to have bells) but were obliged to dress from neck to ankle and waist in black.

'Today, it seems like a piece of cockeyed thinking that in order to escape notice of the local constabulary all 100 riders in a time-trial should wear black tights and black alpaca jacket,' says Bernard Thompson. But, absurd or not, the secrecy survived into the 1960s, although the black wraiths of 'inconspicuous' cycling had by then moved into shorter and more colourful clothes.

The greatest absurdity came when Britain ran the World Championships in 1922. For the NCU it was not only an honour, but a peace treaty. It had been involved from the start in the first world organisation, the International Cyclists Association, but there had been trouble from the start. England, Scotland and Ireland (but not Wales, which hadn't joined) were registered as separate nations, as they still are in the Commonwealth Games. That seemed logical to Britain but to everyone else it appeared to be bites at an apple.

There was also the French question. France had never been able to live with the NCU's or the ICA's strict definition of amateurism. Its largest body, the Union Vélocipèdique Française, had therefore been left out of the ICA, and accreditation was given instead to the cycling association of a large athletic club. 'But,' said the reporter from *Scottish Cyclist*, 'it no more represents French cyclists than, say, the Edinburgh University CC does Scottish cyclists.' It didn't please France, either. If its real national body couldn't be part of the ICA, it would start a world organisation of its own. In this it had the support of other countries, which were still cross at Britain having so many separate affiliations and, as it happened, so many champions. France and the other nations began making their own arrangements and the next the NCU heard was that the ICA had been abandoned, a new Union Cycliste Internationale had started, and that Britain wasn't part of it. The country which had started international cycling had to spend a year in the cold before applying to join the club which had rejected it.

The UCI's offer to run the world championships was, therefore, an honour. The NCU accepted it would have to run a road-race but said it would be a time-trial. That was difficult, given it had banned time-trialling back in 1888 and prohibited 'any of its officials from officiating or assisting at any road-races'. Luckily, all sorts of coat-turning are possible when rewards are high enough, and a year before the championships the NCU said it didn't mind time-trialling after all.

It gave the organisation to the Anfield Bicycle Club in Liverpool, which only a year earlier had been organising rebel 'road-races' – time-trials – and cocking its fingers at the NCU. For men dedicated to the law and the rules of cycling, the situation couldn't have been more absurd. And, not surprisingly, the championships turned out every bit as crazy.

The Anfield chose the track at New Brighton, across the Mersey. British riders thought it excellent. By world standards, it was awful. It was 586 yards round for a start. The surface of cement and gravel was as good as things got when it was built in 1898, but by 1922 continentals had grown accustomed to better things than this pitted and holed track they were asked to ride. The motor-paced events were taken away before the championships even began, unrideable because of the almost non-existent bankings.

That much they could have tolerated had the cement and gravel not turned treacherous in the rain – even in mild dampness – and Liverpool is one of the wettest cities in England. When the sprinter Piet Moeskops gave it a go after a shower, he 'attempted a trial spin but his machine slipped on the greasy surface and he returned limping slightly and shaking his head,' said the man from the local paper, the *Wallasey and Wirral Chronicle*.

There are reports in *Cycling* of British riders shouting for 'stimulants'. The German cycling paper *Rad Welt* said: 'The English amateurs were full of [drugs]. Owen and Oakes are said to have ridden as if drunk, and all the other amateurs showed every indication that they also had taken dope.'

A new stand at the track had seats for 40,000, but never did more than 8,000 people turn up. The organisers had to advertise in the local papers for businesses prepared to advertise in the programme.

The UCI realised its mistake. Having taken away the motor-pacing, it took away everything else as well. Moeskops never rode New Brighton again because the professional sprint, like the other outstanding events, was held in Paris instead. The final disgrace came when the organisers began refunding tickets for the events they had lost. Disgruntled spectators, some of whom had travelled a long way to be disappointed, spotted they could join queues for more expensive tickets than they held. Money was handed back without question and only a few considered it cheating, given the fiasco.

'The management of the meeting left much to be desired,' said the local paper, doubting that the books could ever have balanced.

The one race that went well was the time-trial, over 100 miles, in Shropshire. The British rode in black to the great amusement of foreign riders. That humour didn't last long. More than 160 kilometres alone is a skill that has to be learned, and the British had learned it. They took the first three places, little Dave Marsh winning by 1:20 to become the first of only two British gold medallists in the men's amateur road-race. Graham Webb in 1967, to save you wondering, was the other one, and we'll get to his story a bit later.

Britain saw Marsh and a podium full of Britons – the other medallists were Charles Burkill and Charlie Davie – as compensation for New Brighton and proof of the superiority of The British Way. The British had known all along that lone racing was the only way to find a champion. It's just that they hadn't had a chance to demonstrate it. The fact that it was the NCU that had denied them and that the Anfield Bicycle Club had been branded rebels for trying to prove just that point seems to have escaped everyone's notice.

And then, glory be, Denmark said it, too, would run the World Championship as a time-trial in 1931. Once more Britain could stamp on foreigners' toes. *Cycling* approved of the selection of Freddy Frost, Len Cave and Frank Southall with F. T. Brown (initials were common) as reserve, and boasted:

IF PERFECTLY FIT
Southall Will Win The World's
Road Championship,
predicts "The Loiterer"

The world's amateur road-race championship is absurdly simple this year … It is, therefore, perfectly easy to jot down the English times, note the best times abroad over the distance, and announce the result long before the starter has given the Danish equivalent for the word 'go'!'

Well, he was disappointed. However bad things had been in 1922, the time-trial at least was immaculate. Britain had had a lot of practice. Others hadn't mastered it. Take the case of the 1912 Olympic road-race in Sweden, for instance. It was run as a 320-kilometre time-trial around Lake Malar. *Cycling* was as enthusiastic then as it was about Denmark, crowing, 'Unpaced, we do not think that any nation possesses a rider equal to Moss or Grubb'. But both were to be as disappointed as 'The Loiterer'.

It began at 2 a.m., which is good for sunlight in Sweden but not conducive to a crowd. Riders started at intervals, but could share the pace if they caught anyone. Pairs can ride faster than individuals and they swept up as they went, creating small bunches. The English team of twelve had little experience of groups, and one rider felt so nervous that he sat on the front and towed the rest along. Then he complained the Americans wouldn't share the work – 'they hung on and would not take their share of pacemaking and endeavored to slip away at the controls,' said the manager, J. F. Ditchman – overlooking the fact that he preferred that they didn't.

What made complaining still more pointless was that the winner, G. R. Lewis, the sole South African, had started in the first three, passed the other two early on and rode the rest of the course alone. He won in 10:42:39 and *Cycling* consoled itself that he was, after all, 'a citizen of the British Empire'. Freddie Grubb came second at 8:25, Leon Meredith fourth at 17:25 after crashing with two others and being both cut by a pedal and walloped in the stomach by some handlebars. Heroically, he had also stopped to pull the Scotsman, Wilson, out of a seven-foot ditch of mud.

The disappointment of Sweden should have done little to raise hopes for neighbouring Denmark. But, as so often, history repeated itself as farce. 'The whole race was as badly organised as a road time-trial could be and was a disgrace,' *Cycling* protested. The event was publicised, the roads weren't closed and anybody could follow the riders. Faster competitors ran into convoys that built up behind slower ones and Southall accepted he had sat on a wheel for twenty miles. Crowds mobbed the timekeeper and he couldn't see the riders. Numbers called in one language were translated several times before they reached him. He missed Southall completely and when British officials said he'd finished in 5:6:26, the timekeeper agreed 5:6 but added 30 seconds as a guess.

Likewise, 'A time was recorded against a competitor's number given as 53,' *Cycling* reported:

About that moment I had myself observed a rider crossing the line carrying the number 66 (Olmo, Italy). Three-quarters of an hour later an Italian delegate approached the timekeeper's table and for some moments completely monopolised the attention of the officials whilst he claimed that Olmo had arrived and that he had crossed the line 'one second after Henry Hansen'.

After some minutes of heated discussion in French, Italian, Danish (and I could not resist saying a word, too), the time previously recorded against 53 was transferred to 66 and Olmo was listed second in the Amateur Road Championship of the world.

29

The next sentence is almost tear-inducing: 'What happened to Number 53, T. Wanzenried, of Switzerland, I cannot say. He is not shown on the finishing list at all.'

Little though the race impressed *Cycling*, it did have a big impression on men from another paper. Gaston Bénac, the beret-wearing sports editor of *Paris-Soir*, had gone to Copenhagen with his colleague Albert Baker d'Isy, a cycling writer who once boasted that ink was in his veins and drank a bottle to prove it. He was immediately sick on the carpet.

The two watched Learco Guerra of Italy win the 170-kilometre professional time-trial at 35.2 kph, beating their own French hope, Ferdinand Le Drogo. They resolved to repeat the race each year in Paris, starting the following year, 1932. It would be publicity for the paper, it would be cheaper than a road-race, and spectators would see stars individually and not in the confusion of a bunch.

Bénac told someone to 'take a day off and find a course around 140 kilometres – and remember, no railway crossings!' Baker d'Isy insisted it was he who was asked whereas René de Latour – never shy of enhancing his own reputation and known to British cyclists for his articles in *Sporting Cyclist* – said it was him.

De Latour recalled: 'With much searching of the maps, I got on the right track and after a few rides of inspection had found the course.' It was round a triangle from Versailles through Rambouillet, Maulette, St-Rémy-les-Chevreuse, Versailles and Boulogne to finish on the Buffalo track where Henri Desgrange, the founder of the Tour de France, became the world's first hour-record holder in 1893. There were three hills, plenty of cobbles, and the last 40 kilometres went through the woods of the Vallée de Chevreuse. It worked out at 142 kilometres, just what was wanted. Baker d'Isy came up with the name Grand Prix des Nations, which gave it such class that it had the status of a world championship. In 1953, slowly aware of what was happening abroad and still delighted at the idea of a world-class time-trial, Britain couldn't resist sending its best.

Ken Joy had turned professional to break road records for Hercules. There was no other way to make money on a bike and working with his brother in the building business 'didn't pay enough to pay for the cycling,' he says. Hercules offered him £20 a week, a fortune, and he grabbed it. 'It was simple pounds, shillings and pence,' he said from his home in Nottingham. Joy came originally from Chatham in Kent; he ended up in Nottingham because during his racing career he met a girl there, a romance he pursued by riding 186 miles each way from Chatham to see her.

Joy's reputation travelled before him – he had broken the 12-hour record a month earlier with, as he remembered it, 476 miles. He was, after all, a professional record-breaker, and even French papers picked him out as a favourite. Outside Rouen, a little-known 19-year-old memorised his name. It paid to know the opposition.

Joy rode his heart out. He was worthy of representing Britain. Sadly for British pride, the slender 19-year-old with a fleshy face and blond hair caught him for sixteen minutes. The boy's name was Jacques Anquetil, and he went on to win the Tour de France five times, all through his time-trialling ability, coupled with holding his own in the mountains. He rode the Grand Prix des Nations nine times and won on each occasion.

Caught not only for sixteen minutes but suffering from the 12-hour record, Joy had a less successful ride. He had gone to Paris with his manager from Hercules, the former time-trialling champion, Frank Southall. The man was a taskmaster, he said:

He'd have me attempting records every ten days. If the wind was blowing one way, he'd have me going for one record, if it was blowing another we'd drive down to Penzance or somewhere and try for something else. I was a nervous wreck.

The Grand Prix des Nations was an upsetting experience. Southall just argued with everyone. He wanted to be the manager on the Continent but Hercules wanted someone else who knew more about the scene there and I could hear them arguing. They'd have the loudhailer on the front of their car and all I could hear as I was riding was their arguing.

The repeated record attempts finally made Joy ill. His stomach ulcerated, which he blames on 'endless hours of very lonely riding, eating the kind of food you eat on record attempts; I was losing a stone after every record, then barely recovering before I had to do another one'. He stopped riding, declined requests to take up timekeeping, and never rode a bike again.

Joy never forgot Anquetil, naturally enough, and remembers being impressed at what he called 'a rather shy boy' training on the course behind a Citroën car the previous day. 'He was really doing a rate of knots.' What's more impressive is that Anquetil never forgot Joy, whom he mentions in his biography. British time-trialling intrigued him – he presented BBAR trophies to Beryl Burton and Brian Kirby at the Albert Hall in 1961 – and he got to talking about it in a French restaurant near Leicester Square on Good Friday 1964.

The restaurant owner hadn't wanted to serve lunch at 11.45 a.m. so Alan Gayfer, the editor of *Cycling*, explained that his guests couldn't eat later because they were due at Herne Hill in the afternoon and that, regrettably, 'Monsieur Anquetil will have to eat somewhere else.' The man gasped '*Mon dieu!*' and said 11.45 would be no problem.

The other guest was the British star Tom Simpson, who had ridden many time-trials before leaving for France in 1959. The three spoke of British racing and Anquetil's ability at time-trialling and Anquetil said that he'd like to try a '25' on the Southend road, then the fastest course in the country. Gayfer asked what time he'd do. Simpson broke in to say that courses were pretty flat, that they finished where they started and so there was as much tail-wind as head-wind, that they rose and fell no more than 70 metres, and there was no more climbing than descending. Anquetil said he thought he'd do it in 46 minutes.

The others had given him no guidance. In fact, the record was 54:23, to Bas Breedon. With no guidance, he had estimated eight minutes less than the fastest '25' ever ridden. The conversation then turned more serious. A deal was looking possible. Anquetil asked for £1,000, and a London timber merchant and bike enthusiast called Vic Jenner, who'd ridden the 1932 World Championship in Italy at his own expense, said he'd put up the money. Anquetil remained keen but Jenner died shortly afterwards and it never happened.

The 25-mile record, by the way, didn't fall below Anquetil's estimate until Chris Boardman lowered it to 45:57 in 1993. It had taken three decades.

.4

STRANGE TALES FROM ABROAD

So, did anybody ride road-races in those days? Surprisingly, the answer is yes, they did – although at first always abroad.

The big name of the era was George Mills, who at 19 set the second record from Land's End to John o'Groats. The first holder was J. Lennox (such is fame that his first name is forgotten), who bounced behind pacing tandems for six days and sixteen hours in 1885. The next year Mills, not even 20, rode the event twice, once on a bicycle and once on a trike. As Bidlake said: 'The sensation was not that he was merely one of a sequence of record breakers, but that he knocked more than a day off each of the previous bests, in a sort of double event, riding virtually without sleep, certainly with no more than a wayside nod.'

In an age when the record stands at much less than two days, it's hard to grasp the significance of Mills doing it in around five, and that with the help of pacers. But Mills rode a penny-farthing without convincing brakes. Imagine that, going down a Scottish mountain at night after half a week without sleep. Mills also took the 24-hour record, at one time holding it on a penny-farthing, a modern-style 'safety', a tricycle, and also on a tandem bicycle and a tandem tricycle. He was quite a bloke. And just the man to send to the first Bordeaux–Paris in 1891.

The organiser was the newspaper *Véloce-Sport*, which mixed sport with general news and a lot of opinion. The involvement of a newspaper was no surprise because organising long races was the only publicity they could create. To send men impossible distances on unsurfaced roads not only fired the imagination and created heroes, but nobody could know what happened without buying a paper.

The British said they'd ride the pioneering event if the French would promise no professionals would take part. The French idea of an amateur was anyone who earned no more than a living wage from sport. Provided you didn't become stinking rich at it, you were an amateur. The British said that was no good, that a definition like that would corrupt their amateur status and the organisers were so thrilled to see them ride that they changed their rules. They also went to great lengths to make sure all went well, to the extent of laying on beds and meals for the two days they thought it would take to get from the south-west coast to the capital. In fact, it took Mills 26 hours, riding on a diet that included a great many strawberries, and British riders took the first four places. The beds were unused although the French were reported to be impressed at how much of their food the British got through.

Any organisation other than the NCU would have been delighted. The NCU, though, called Mills to an inquiry. He was a foreman at the Humber bike factory in Beeston, near Nottingham, they said, and how did they know that Humber hadn't paid his fare? Mills was forced to prove he paid his own way and only then would the NCU grudgingly accept that he hadn't had a penny from his employer and therefore hadn't made himself a professional.

Within a few years the NCU had a much more blatant case to deal with. Arthur Linton rode – and also won – Bordeaux–Paris in the 1896 race. It started on Saturday, 23 May and this time there was no fuss about amateurism. Linton was there to win what he could and he hired a highly controversial trainer – what we'd now call a *soigneur* – called Choppy Warburton.

Warburton was known to the authorities. To start with he had been a professional runner, a 'pedestrian', which meant more than it said. Professional running was a rough-house and a breeding ground for the dubious. Betting was rife and so, many said, was race-fixing. He left running in 1873 and became full-time coach to Manchester Athletic Club. Neither his running background nor his job in Manchester was what the NCU went in for and it, too, declared Warburton a professional. That meant he couldn't race on the track but he could indeed exercise his craft there.

Even now, nobody knows if he was a con man or a great dope king. He looked the shaky svengali, all knowing smiles, long overcoats and curly brimmed bowlers. The Anglo-American writer and cleric Dick Swann, writing of him, said: 'Choppy was, as befits any pro manager, a sharp dresser and flamboyant personality, given to extra-long topcoats with many pockets, and gaudy waistcoats. Where pro cycling ruled the roost, as in France, Germany and the USA, this was acceptable. But in England, the home of the Gentleman Amateur, he was heartily disliked, feared and in fact hated by the National Cyclists Union.'

The *Cycling Gazette* of Chicago called him 'undoubtedly the most widely-advertised figure in European cycle-racing circles; his every movement created talk.' *Paris-Vélo* said:

He is everywhere at the same time, never in the same place. In the track centre he is the only one you see, his great overcoat and his derby hat pushed down to his ears with a bang of his fist. He gives out an air of mystery that intrigues rivals and thrills the public.

From his pocket he suddenly takes a small glass container, shows it to his rider, uncorks it with dramatic care, pours the unknown mixture that it contains into a milk bottle and, still running, knocking over anyone who gets in the way, gets himself to the other side of the track to pass it to [his rider].'

It's a drug, say some, just bluff say others; but drug or bluff, it's all the same.

Warburton's job was to get Linton through the Bordeaux–Paris of 1896 and to overcome the French favourite, a nattily bearded Frenchman called Gaston Rivierre. The two differed in every way, but particularly in tactics. Linton chose an aggressive style to wear the Frenchman down, to which Rivierre retaliated by riding constantly at the same speed, allowing Linton to burn himself out. Which he did, at a record speed of 27.7 kph.

The man from *Cyclers' News*, calling himself 'one who knows', said of that year's race: 'I saw him at Tours, half way through the race, at midnight, where he came in with glassy eyes and tottering limbs, and in a high state of nervous excitement. I then heard him swear – a very rare occurrence with him – but after a rest he was off again, though none of us expected he would go very far. At Orléans at five o'clock in the morning, Choppy and I looked after a wreck – a corpse as Choppy called him – yet he had sufficient energy, heart, pluck, call it what you will, to enable him to gain 18 minutes on the last 45 miles of hilly road.'

Choppy Warburton was there, magic bottle to hand, flogging the last life from his corpse.

Even in his awful state, Linton must have tried to understand the cheers of the crowd at the Vélodrome de Seine. He seemed to have won; yet he knew that Rivierre was ahead of him. What had happened was that Linton's pacers had taken the wrong bridge across the Seine, cutting off only a few kilometres but bypassing Rivierre, who'd reached Paris second but gone the right way. The judges declared the race a tie. Third man, Marius Thé, arrived 55 minutes later. Riders were still coming in for another day.

Word of Linton's dreadful condition started to spread. *Sporting Life* reported: 'I hear by a side wind that one eminent promoter of professionalism could a tale unfold which would cause each individual hair upon the Licensing Committee of the NCU to stand on end.' What *Sporting Life* heard of this 'promoter of professionalism' – undoubtedly Warburton – was that Linton had been kept going with strychnine, trimethyl or heroin, possibly all three.

Linton died nine weeks later, on 23 July, 1896 at home in Aberdare, Wales. He had typhoid fever. *Cyclers' News* decided on 28 July, 1896 that 'the gigantic effort Linton made in the Bordeaux to Paris race undermined his constitution, and gave him little strength to battle against the fever'.

Warburton, meanwhile, had become engrossed in another scandal, this time involving Jimmy Michael, the baby-faced, pint-sized sprinter who was both the biggest earner in cycling and Britain's first World Champion. Once more drugs appeared to be involved and the most lurid tales tell of Michael being so strung up that he fell repeatedly off his bike and climbed back on to start racing the wrong way round the track. Whatever the truth, the NCU reputedly banned Warburton from every track in Britain – 'reputedly' because the NCU and later the British Cycling Federation has no record of a ban.

Arthur Linton and 'Choppy' Warburton at Herne Hill

Whatever it was that happened, Warburton left for Germany in 1897 – the 'ban' didn't apply there – and he managed the Frenchman Albert Champion, an early Classics winner and founder of the Champion spark-plug company. But his life was as ruined as the riders he helped. Warburton died in Wood Green, north London, on 17 December that same year, aged 54.

Bryan Wotton, once racing secretary of the BCF and later the organiser of drug tests for the International Amateur Athletics Federation, says:

> I have my own strange vision of the Warburton era. This was a time when Cucca [a preparation that included cocaine] was endorsed by the Cyclists' Touring Club and when a British supplier lent its name and no doubt financial support to the Cucca Cup races. Thus if Choppy was not around or his case of magic potions was misplaced, the riders could always turn to the Cucca stand and obtain a little something to take them through the night.
>
> During my time at the BCF I spent many fruitless hours reading minutes of the various committees in an endeavour to discover the exact nature of Warburton's offences. I believe that he was banned from entering *any* racing enclosure and therefore the judgement was unlikely to have been made by anything other than a national committee, but there was not one single mention.
>
> I can only assume that he was unofficially warned off. As they had no doping regulations, the offence was probably 'bringing the sport into disrepute'.

And there the mystery remains. Dope fiend or confidence king, banned for life or just asked to stay away? And why did someone at the time decide that no record should be kept of the fate of such an enigmatic and colourful character? We shall never know.

5

SECRET SUCCESS

The great years of time-trialling produced a man to match them. He was Frank Southall, all round-faced with thick hair brushed up and back without a parting. I've never met anyone who said he was likeable, but maybe that wasn't necessary. Ken Joy, whom Southall managed when Hercules had a record-breaking team, told me: 'You didn't want to upset him or you knew it. He wasn't a pleasant man. If he smiled, you watched his eyes, not his mouth.'

In April 1930 the magazine *Cycling* started its British Best All-Rounder competition, a season-long championship averaging riders' best speeds at 50 and 100 miles, and 12 hours. Southall won the opening championship in 21.141 mph and signed the *Golden Book of Cycling* the following year. His entry says: 'Southall holds the world's unpaced standing start track records at one, five, ten and twenty miles. He also holds 28 national track records. On the road he has won every classic open event, including hill-climbs, making competition records at 25, 50 and 100 miles.'

In fact, he was rarely beaten from 1925 to 1933, including the first four BBAR competitions in a row. Bernard Thompson called him 'a superman in time-trial sport'.

Southall could win at 12 hours – 236 miles in his first BBAR – and he was virtually unbeatable in a 4,000-metre pursuit. He came sixth to Attilio Pavesi of Italy in the 1932 Olympic road-race in Los Angeles. But that was the last to be run as a time-trial; the change to a massed-start race from 1936 committed Britain to international darkness. The Olympic torch had gone out. *Cycling*, which saw anything but time-trialling and track racing as almost corrupt and immoral, complained:

The strongest possible protest ought to be made by the English delegates both to the UCI and the Olympic committees against the recent decision by the UCI that the Olympic road-race for 1936 is to be a massed-start affair. The Olympic Games were the last stronghold of the genuine international trial of road-riding ability, free from tactics or bunching.

Southall turned professional in 1934 for place-to-place records. He broke nine in two years but a great talent had been squandered. He should have been internationally famous. Instead he was an anonymous figure in black, denied public adulation by the rules of his own sport.

Frank Southall on the Catford Hill Climb

The change in attitudes started on 17 June 1933 when the Charlotteville club at Guildford in Surrey organised a massed-start race on the Brooklands car circuit, a place better known for huge racing Bentleys with spoked wheels and strapped-down bonnets. The organiser was Vic Jenner, the man who wanted to pay Jacques Anquetil to ride on the Southend road. The business manager was Bill Mills, with whom Jenner had ridden in the 1932 World Championship, and whose despair at *Cycling*'s enmity to road-racing led him to start a rival magazine, *The Bicycle*, in 1937.

The NCU supported the event because it wasn't on the road. It even said it would pick its World Championship team on the results. And so the gloriously named 100-kilometre Massed-Start World's Cycling Championship Trial was started at 4 p.m. by Sir Malcolm Campbell, the hero of the time, who set nine speed records on land and three on water, all in vehicles called Bluebird. The programme explained that a twenty-guinea trophy put up by *Cycling* would be presented by Miss Betty Fields, sister of the singer Gracie Fields, and by the boxer Jack Doyle. It warned that the list of riders' names was copyright 'and any person found making illegal use thereof will be prosecuted'.

There were 102 on the start-sheet and 10,000 in the crowd despite the rain. The race was like kick-and-rush football, tactics limited to random and eccentric attacking by the best, hanging on for most.

Only 64 remained by the end of three laps. *Cycling* concluded: 'You cannot teach time-trial Englishmen to change their tactics with a single race. Team co-operation was conspicuous by its absence.' The winner, Jack Salt, 'rode almost in the same way as he would tackle a time-trial, except that, naturally, he took advantage of such pace as was available in the groups he rode with'.

Among the riders was a piping-voiced man called Percy Stallard, who was born above his father's shabby bike shop in Broad Street, Wolverhampton, on 19 July 1909 and lived there almost to his death. He'd never ridden a massed-start race and two punctures made sure he didn't finish. But he did win several primes – intermediate prizes for the first up a hill – and that was enough for the NCU to pick him for the World Championship.

Decades later I went to see him in his bike shop, a dark and cluttered place where it didn't surprise me to see a cardboard box labelled 'Osgear spares'. Osgears hadn't been made since I was a boy. Stallard turned out to be a short, stocky man with a round, shining face with bright, almost rodent-like eyes and a smile as sharp as his observations. He told me:

The test hill [the main climb, used for testing cars, which officials said was 25 per cent] that you had to go up five times was that steep that on the first lap I pulled my foot out of my toeclips and I ran up. I was in the lead then and several other riders passed me. Well, I couldn't get back on my bike at that steep angle, so I *ran* past these other riders and won the prime at the top, *running*!

That happened for the next two times. I won three laps like that, running up a hill in a cycle race. It's farcical, really. And another thing that happened: my tyre was going down. And I pumped it up – it wasn't flat – and got to the pits, and I'd just put a new front wheel in and the commissaire came running up saying 'You can't do that, you can't do that; you've got to change the tyre'. I had to take the wheel back out and put the tyre back on on my own. That's how they did things in those days.

It got that Stallard could change a tyre, pump it up and set off again in a minute and ten seconds. 'I was the first one to be selected for a championship on other than time-trial performance,' he reckoned:

Cycling, who used to run the Best All-Rounder competition in those days, they were that indignant that anyone like me should be selected that in their report, when they announced the team, they said the team for the World Championship was Southall from London, Salt from Liverpool and 'someone from the Midlands to give geographical balance'.

And the fact that I was the first Englishman to finish in the World Championship, in eleventh position, meant nothing to them. *Cycling* in those days thought that a bunched race was just a question of hanging on and winning the sprint at the finish, no more than that.

Of the others at the World Championship, Frank Southall's speed got him into the leading group of the 38 starters, but lack of experience showed on each rise of the shallow Montlhèry car circuit where the race was held. There, says Chas Messenger in his book *Ride and Be Damned*: 'You could see the difference between our time-triallists and the Continentals; we tended to steamroller over it while the Continentals honked up [rode out of the saddle] and so on every lap, once over the top, our lads had to make up the leeway.' Southall abandoned after problems with his two-speed gears; Salt came 21st and last.

A year later the NCU sent Stallard, his fellow-Midlander Charlie Holland, and Fred Ghilks to Leipzig. Like the others, Stallard had no training clothes and went out in khaki shorts and shirt. The nattily dressed Continentals nicknamed him 'Boy Scout'.

Holland rode a single 81-inch gear in the race and was left for dead in fourth place when the other three in the break clicked up through their derailleur gears for the sprint. Stallard and Ghilks didn't finish for another two minutes, Stallard coming seventh and Ghilks 26th and last. The winner was Kees Pellenaars, who became the Dutch Tour de France manager during the 1950s and 1960s, and the man who single-handedly kept Dutch professional racing going in that period. Charlie Holland, on the other hand, went on to become the first Briton to last more than a single stage of the Tour.

Other than the few who had ridden abroad, few riders had much idea of what to expect. In June 1936 the Isle of Man, a separate country with nothing to fear from the police, ran a race over a lap of the TT circuit. Riders now had to manage real-life streets that twisted and turned. Eight came down in the first few hundred yards. Four more fell at five miles when a lorry on the course led two riders to change direction. A rider hit a motorcycle and side-car at Quarter Bridge, and there was another spill at Glen Helen.

Two more fell off near Kirk Michael. Another ten crashed after Ballacraine after someone's chain broke. Further riders crashed at The Bungalow, two at Keppel Gate, and at Creg-ny-Baa. A Londoner, Reg Green, missed the sandbags protecting a corner, hit a stone wall and broke his nose. Another jammed his chain as he went round Governors Bridge and ran the last mile with his bike. In all 31 riders fell off in 38 miles, and that from a field of 81. Only 48 finished, two riders had broken collar-bones and six needed hospital treatment.

It was an appalling start, but it was road-racing as we know it. Or almost, anyway.

6

AND, THEREFORE, THIS COUNTRY
IS AT WAR...

... with Germany, is what Neville Chamberlain told the nation on 3 September 1939. Members of my old CTC district in west London remember hearing the news during a club run, while they were drinking tea at Chenies, in Buckinghamshire. One, Eric Jefferies, recalled: 'A kind of shock came over everyone. We all smoked, even those that normally didn't. The run was abandoned and we all went slowly home.'

But pretty soon cycling was at war with itself.

In December 1941, Stallard contacted another national leader with a similar name, A. P. Chamberlin of the National Cyclists' Union. 'I can never understand why massed-start racing is not indulged on the public roads of this country,' he wrote:

> It is amazing to think that this is the only country in Europe where this form of sport is not permitted ... There seems to be the mistaken idea that it would be necessary to close the roads. This, of course, is entirely wrong ... There would be no better time than now to introduce this form of racing to the roads, what with decreased amount of motor traffic and the important part that the cycle is playing in wartime transport.

Unlike Chamberlain, Chamberlin was in no mood for appeasement. Like Chamberlain, Stallard reluctantly decided the time had come for war. Circuit-racing, he realised, would never be better than second-best. Now the government had taken airfield and car circuits for the Air Force anyway, the only place left for Stallard's plans was the road. With pleasing drama, he called a meeting at the foot of Long Mynd in Shropshire on Easter Monday 1942 and revealed his plans for a 59-mile race from Llangollen to

Wolverhampton. There would be 40 riders, he said, any profit would go to the Wolverhampton *Express and Star* Forces Comfort Fund, and, more significantly, the police along the route had given their approval. The date was set for 7 June and Stallard went home to Wolverhampton to write letters of invitation on his bike-shop note paper.

'I just explained to the police what I was doing and told them that things like that were normal on the Continent,' he told me, 'and they said they were happy and that they'd try to help.'

It didn't convince George Herbert Stancer, one of the sport's beasts of the jungle and a man of great influence. He was old enough to remember the time-trial breakaway from the NCU in 1897, and he approved it because it had been 'fought out in the council chamber'. The Stallard rebellion was different, he argued, although in fact much the same had happened: just as the time-trial rebels had had no satisfaction with the NCU, so Stallard had got nowhere with them either.

Percy Stallard – the inspiration behind the BLRC

What really worried Stancer wasn't whether democracy and discussion were involved, nor whether road-racing would threaten all cycling. That worry had long passed. His point was that time-trials, being secret and supposedly illegal, had never sought police permission. The police had done nothing to stop them but there was always the fear on the RTTC's part that if promoters asked permission, they'd be forced to say no. Better, therefore, not to ask. It was all very civic-minded of Stallard to invite police co-operation but it was a boat that the RTTC didn't want rocked. To ask permission was to concede that permission was needed and that acknowledged that the police had the right to refuse.

Stancer explained all that in *Cycling* under the headline 'A HOPELESS REVOLT'. He wrote:

> They have plunged into their dangerous experiment without regard for the consequences ... I understand that the 'rebels' want to go on holding races by police permit and under police protection; and when this is withdrawn they are apparently content to put up the shutters and go out of business as promoters.
>
> Our sport, as practised by the RTTC, is not illegal. It does not need a police permit, and it is the worst possible policy to ask for one. If we voluntarily place road-racing under police control, we sign its death warrant ... If we are to race on the road, for heaven's sake let us do it as free citizens, and not by permission of the police.

The NCU took its lead from Stancer. It suspended Stallard even before he'd run the race. It offered him a way out if he'd attend a meeting on 2 May, where presumably the price would have been to abandon his plans, but Stallard stayed away. The RTTC's agreement with the NCU meant that his suspension applied also to time-trialling.

On the day, though, *Cycling* had no choice but to cover the story. It was too big to ignore. 'BIG CROWD AT FINISH OF BANNED RACE' said its headline. The report started:

More than a thousand people watched the finish of the massed-start race organised by Percy Stallard, from Llangollen to Wolverhampton, on Sunday afternoon. The Chief Constable of Wolverhampton, an inspector, a sergeant and 15 uniformed policemen kept the crowd back. Police cars and police motorcyclists patrolled portions of the course. A police motorcyclist led the racing men through the streets to the finish. E. A. Price, of Wolverhampton, won the sprint from his clubmate, C. J. Anslow.

The rest pointed out that the race had been banned by the NCU and RTTC, that there had been no incidents other than a lorry backing on to the course, and that the time of 'approximately 2hrs 2mins for the 59 miles [was] a fast ride in excellent weather conditions'.

The fifteen riders who finished the course then went off to Wolverhampton Wanderers' football grounds to change and shower. The result:

1.	Albert Price	Wolverhampton	2:25:40
2.	Cec Anslow	Wolverhampton	2:25:41
3.	Jack Holmes	RAF	2:26:23
4.	J. Kremers	Royal Dutch Brigade	2:26:33
5.	E. Whitmore	RAF	2:26:35
6.	R. Jones	Wolverhampton	2:26:36
7.	S. Trubshaw	Wolverhampton	2:26:40
8.	E. Turner	Wolverhampton	2:26:45
9.	R. Whitmore	RAF	2:29:10
10.	E. Reddish	RAF	2:29:10

Anslow, by the way, was riding a fixed wheel.

Having already suspended Stallard, the NCU then suspended everyone else as well – riders and officials alike, almost 50 in all. The logic was impeccable, but the consequences inevitable. Create outlaws and they'll live outside the law. They have no way back unless you, too, back down. And the NCU, supported by the RTTC and then by *Cycling*, wasn't about to do that.

The race had been on 7 June. On 12 July Wolverhampton RCC called a meeting of 60 members of local clubs 'to control cycling sport in all its branches' through a new organisation. A second road-race, the Circuit of the Wrekin (won by Ernie Clements, later manager of the Falcon semi-professional team), took place on 2 August, followed by more suspensions, this time including three entire clubs. After the Circuit of the Wrekin came Morecambe–Bradford on 16 August , also won by Clements (with the future millionaire bike-dealer Ron Kitching third, running across the line after falling on the cobbles of Manningham Lane), and the Craven Dales race on 27 September, which Stallard won with Clements second.

There were further breakaway meetings in Yorkshire and in London, where Bill Mills – business manager of the Charlotteville races and editor of *The Bicycle* – was elected chairman and one of his writers, Peter Bryan, who with great irony was years later to become managing editor of the very anti-road-racing *Cycling*, as treasurer.

Some 67 riders were now outside the NCU and clubs were even starting to run time-trials outside the RTTC. At 10.45 a.m. on 15 November 1942, those who could find the money and petrol coupons to get to Buxton youth hostel met there to form their new organisation. The proposal that it should be called the British League of Racing Cyclists came from the vice-chairman J. E. Finn, finisher number 6 in the pioneering Llangollen–Wolverhampton. The meeting ended at 4.15 p.m., one of the shortest and least rowdy the infant organisation would ever have.

Stallard went home with the title of BLRC event organiser, but he was the spirit if not the true leader of the new organisation. In his private papers, he described the league as 'a one-man effort with the intermittent help of Charlie Fox, "Stoppa" Clarke, Jimmy Kain, Ralph Jones and Len Hook'.

Running the BLRC wasn't easy for anyone. It was an organisation of rebels, troublemakers, pioneers, visionaries, misfits, international socialists, jazz beats and anyone else who cared to join. 'There were a lot more misfits than there were fitters,' said Peter Bryan, who'd covered Llangollen–Wolverhampton for *The Bicycle*. In 1943 the

BLRC expelled even Stallard for saying some organisers weren't as good as they ought to be. The remark (perhaps even true) was judged 'conduct detrimental to the league's interest' and the BLRC's godfather was thrown out of his own organisation for a year.

It seems an almost crazy thing to do but it would have been an easy decision for many to take, says Bryan. Stallard had an ability to make enemies even of those determined to be friends, he remembers. 'Stallard had the most abrasive nature that I have ever met,' he said slowly, for emphasis. 'He could never believe that he could have a bad idea or make a bad decision. And sometimes he'd go berserk with those who disagreed with him. He didn't have, let us say, the delicacies of negotiation.' Despite that, Bryan resigned from the BLRC in protest at Stallard's suspension. It was all part of the hurly-burly of an organisation founded through rebellion and conducted by rebels.

Jimmy Kain wrote from his home in Hastings of 'the two years of nervous and physical breakdown that followed six years of BLRC office'. Not that it shortened his life: he died in 1983 aged 99, the oldest resident of the Chelsea Royal Hospital, having been starter of the World Professional Road-Race Championship at Goodwood the previous summer.

What happened next must have made sense at the time. As a list, it just looks confusing and self-contradictory. On 13 September 1943 the Home Secretary, Herbert Morrison, said road-races were 'likely not only to cause obstruction to traffic but to be a source of danger both to the public and the racers'. On 3 November the NCU and RTTC dropped their suspensions of BLRC members, while still not supporting road-races. On 8 December the BLRC met the Ministry of Transport and said it had persuaded it to change its mind. On 12 January 1944 the RTTC said its clubs should expel members who belonged to the BLRC. Scotland (where informal road-races had in any case been held between the wars) went ahead with a ban at the end of the month and the RTTC refused membership to Bradford RCC because it had run road-races.

As if all this weren't muddled enough, *Cycling* said in 1944 that it no longer opposed BLRC races and now planned to report them. Harry England, the editor from 1929 to 1959 (and who on trains travelled first class on expenses while demanding his staff sat in third class), considered the RTTC had stabbed him in the back. The magazine had started the British Best All-Rounder competition in 1930, and had seen that, and itself, as the corner-stone of the sport. It was that authoritative stance which had brought its opposition to the rebel BLRC and the threat it represented not only to cycling but *Cycling*.

In 1944, though, the RTTC said it was going to run a BBAR of its own. It would be over 25, 50 and 100 miles instead of the now classic distances of the *Cycling* competition (50, 100 and 12 hours), but that was only because riders lacked racing and training because of the war. Whether Harry England liked it or not, the sport and the organisation he had spent his life supporting had snatched away the very means by which he'd done it. Now, anxious to seek friends where once there had been only enemies, he ended his letter to Charlie Fox, organiser of the first national road-race championship, 'Hope you are fit and well, and with all good wishes'. It was the most extraordinary letter Fox had received.

Much happened within and outside the BLRC, and for a while it looked as though the UCI would recognise it as Britain's international body. But civil wars are exhausting of both men and money. As well as that, the BLRC seemed intent on fighting an internal as well as an external war. Ron Kitching, who'd been a member from the start, said: 'Any rebel movement attracts rebellious characters and the whole thing became a mess.'

Peter Bryan, later editor of *The Bicycle*, said: 'The BLRC was originally a gang of enthusiasts. Then along came what I'd call the parliamentarians of pedal power, men who saw a runaway organisation and decided they'd take it over.'

The BLRC, which had never had worthwhile funds, teetered repeatedly close to bankruptcy, and the NCU, too, grew poorer and poorer as it fought its own fight. There were claims and counter-claims of what each side was supposed to have done, the sabotage it had organised, the lobbying it had carried out with parliamentarians and ministry offices. To this day probably nobody knows how much is true and what was just wild claim, rumour, supposition, or bitter retaliation.

The RTTC, which had no offices, no paid officials and no responsibilities beyond compiling calendars and rules, came out of the war as strong as it had gone in. BLRC clubs had run occasional time-trials, but to the RTTC they had been no more than biting fleas. Stalemate was approaching, exhaustion was already rampant and bankruptcy loomed. It needed men of good will to find a way out.

In 1954 Chas Fearnley wrote in the BLRC's magazine, *The Leaguer*, that 'there is a malignant ulcer prevalent in the cycling world and common to all three racing bodies in this country. It is the taint of vanity and culminates in the clash of personality'. In other words, for some the battle was a cause in itself. Conciliation was no longer the prize.

'In the end,' said Stallard, 'even the NCU started running races on the road ... The NCU were running road-races and we were running road-races *and there wasn't any need for amalgamation at all.'* Stallard, therefore, was firmly in the 'cause in itself camp'. The BLRC had come about because nobody else would run road-racing. It was road-racing that was the aim, not the establishment of the BLRC. Once the battle had been won, it didn't matter who ran it; the one thing that nobody wanted, except Stallard and perhaps a couple of others, was two organisations running rival calendars.

In 1958, penniless and as exhausted as the NCU, the BLRC agreed 'that all assets, liabilities, obligations and commitments of the British League of Racing Cyclists should be transferred or handed over to the British Cycling Federation'. On 1 February 1959 the BCF came into existence, the BLRC and the NCU vanished, and the war was over. Still steaming on as ever, as the smoke cleared, was the great battleship of the RTTC.

Stallard never forgave those who signed away his league. 'It was brought about by the apathy of the membership,' he told me. 'We had three people in particular who thought we should have agreement with the NCU. There was the chairman and a fella named Thompson from Sheffield and someone else.'

As bitter with the BLRC he had created as with the NCU he had helped defeat, he said: 'I would never again try to achieve the impossible by trying to change the order of things. On the two occasions I have tried to do this [the other was a change in racing for riders over 40], I have failed, not because I lacked followers or because of the opposition of opposing bodies, but because of the activities of anarchists and those who are envious of your successes and popularity. Life has taught me that one should never expect appreciation for efforts, whatever they may be.'

Nor did he forgive the new BCF. In March 1988 he refused to go to a BCF dinner where he had been invited to receive the federation's gold medal. 'The significance of the award is nil as it does not open the locked doors of the BCF to me or anyone else with progressive ideas,' he told the secretary, Len Unwin.

Just before his death on 11 August 2001, Stallard wrote to me:

The life suspension inflicted upon me by the NCU is still very much in evidence, whatever the BCF may say. If this is not so, why did they never ask me to manage a British team abroad? After all, I am the only person to have led a British team to individual and team success in the Warsaw–Berlin–Prague [the Peace Race] and then again as the only official accompanying and directing four riders against a team of 117 Mexicans [Tour of Mexico, 1952]; our third individual and third team was equal to our WBP achievement.

When I came to write an obituary for the *Daily Telegraph*, I couldn't help opening with the words that Stallard had been a far-sighted, difficult, argumentative sod, who in the end fell out with everyone he ever dealt with, but whose commitment, enthusiasm and bravery had brought British cycling into the twentieth century and quite possibly saved it.

The appeal that the BLRC had has outlived Stallard. There is a BLRC Association and men with grey hair and slightly stooped walks still wear the league's round badge at reunions. Their nostalgia is encouraged by younger riders who remember little of the bitterness, the sabotage of races by spreading tacks and turning arrows, the sometimes lifelong contempt between fellow cyclists that the conflict produced. They remember only the excitement of life on the edge of the precipice, the feeling of hindsight glory that they had been rebels with a cause.

Getting the era into perspective is easy if all that matters – and obviously that does matter a great deal – is the introduction of road-racing. But it's harder if, even dismissing hindsight, you try to work out why so many intelligent men on both sides could have such mutually opposing views.

John Dennis, still active at Reading track, worked for *The Bicycle*, the short-lived but fondly remembered rival to *Cycling* which was as accepting of the BLRC as *Cycling* was against it. He was an amateur who formed a professional cycling league – of which more later – and yet he was an NCU member so that he could race on the track, where the League had little influence. He told the Fellowship of Cycling Old-timers:

> What has been lost beneath the clouds of myths surrounding the situation is the reason why many clubs were cautious about wholeheartedly supporting the road-racing movement. Remember that it was wartime, and the younger membership of most clubs was away engaged in a war. The older members left at home did not wish to risk damaging a sport which all had enjoyed while their clubmates were away, so they decided to maintain the status quo until the servicemen returned.

And then the other question is what would have happened had Stallard not run his race and the BLRC not been formed. Would there have been road-racing in Britain in time anyway? Peter Bryan's view, detached from the rosy-eyed memory of men who fought a rebellion and won, is that there probably wouldn't. 'The NCU and the RTTC were never friends,' he said. 'The RTTC were particular bastards and they had so many clever men in the top echelon, many more than the NCU. They were steeped in the tradition of time-trialling and what it stood for and they wouldn't budge a jot or tickle.'

The big change came when the UCI told Britain to sort itself out, or be excluded from world cycling, and when it said it would recognise both the BLRC and the NCU. Until then the NCU had had the master card, that whatever happened at home, only it could select teams for world championships and only it could speak for

Britain east of Dover. The UCI was aware of the way things were going and that the BLRC, although perhaps not made up of the nicest of people, was closer to its ideals of international cycling than the well-intentioned but highly cautious UCI.

'That was a serious threat,' Peter Bryan says, 'and the NCU had to do something about it, which is why they eased their opposition. Otherwise they would have lived alongside the RTTC and there would have been no road-racing, not without the BLRC. You can never say that if that didn't happen then this wouldn't have happened, but I can't see what else [other than the BLRC] would have brought it about.'

It stands to reason that there must have been some who were against road-racing because they disliked the idea, or were convinced the police would intervene and then clamp down on all cycling. Others, like the man who became editor of *Sporting Cyclist*, Jock Wadley, believed that if continental racing came to Britain it would have killed British cycling. 'He had seen the way the race caravans acted in France,' said Peter Bryan, 'and the way they just had no respect for personal property and said, "We're the race and we're coming through" and he knew what would happen in Britain if we saw the same thing, although he later changed his views.'

After that came the suspicion of surrendering control of a legal sport to the police, as Stancer explained.

All those reasons are respectable, the first a matter of choice, the second wrong only with hindsight, the third quite reasonable. You can hardly blame someone – in this case the NCU and the RTTC – for not wanting others to ruin their sport. Nor can you feel superior because you know how the story ended. That's what makes the story so unsatisfying.

7

ROAD TO VICTORY

Well, then … would it have happened anyway? Would road-racing have started after the war anyway? Did it need the empty roads of war to do it? Did the war itself contribute to the frustration that made it happen? All of those, probably. But it doesn't matter. History is what happened, not what might have happened if William the Conqueror had never landed.

The first thing that happened is that road-racing took off. The first national championship was run in 1943 under the slogan 'the hardest cycle race ever organised in Great Britain'. It began and ended in Harrogate, 25 riders took part (BLRC membership, while noisy, and seeming larger, was only 450), and a quoted 1,000 people watched Ernie Clements beat Dick Boyden by a length after 72 miles.

The second is that over August bank holiday the following year the Southern Grand Prix in Kent became Britain's first stage-race. Stallard won the first stage and came second on the third and last but the time he lost on the second stage meant that the race was won by Les Plume of Manchester

The third followed a further year later, when the Victory Cycling Marathon – the first Tour of Britain – was run in 1945. And the fourth was that in 1946 riders started riding with advertising on their jerseys, so-called independents or semi-professionals riding openly against amateurs.

The national stage race was to have started in London and gone to Glasgow in four days. In fact there was a question mark over both ends. In the south, the London end of the BLRC wanted the race to start in Brighton; enthusiasts in the Midlands thought London was far enough south, but lost the battle. Scotland was a different problem. There'd never been any doubt about whether the race would finish in Glasgow, only over whether there was enough BLRC-like enthusiasm there to make it happen.

Scotland didn't then have its own association, the Scottish Cycling Union. It belonged to the very English NCU, an organisation literally in another country. In Scotland, the threat to cycling had never been perceived as it had in England, the laws, customs and the density of population being different, and there had in fact been some road-races run there, outside the NCU's control.

The news that Britain was to have a race approaching the flavour of the Tour de France, if not its length or quality, created enough enthusiasm in Scotland for twelve clubs to leave the NCU. Any remaining doubt about whether the race would be well supported there was gone.

Chas Messenger, in his history of the BLRC, says: 'No one had ever put on a stage-race in this country, other than the Southern Grand Prix, and even fewer people had ever seen one. So raw were they that Jimmy Kain [the organiser] even wrote to the Autocycle Union [the body for car-racing] and the flags used by them were taken as a guide to what would be needed.'

The whole event depended on riders finding spare beds in their homes as the race passed through their area. The rules neutralised the race every time it passed through a town or village, where riders were told to ride in single file. They were to bring all the shorts they owned and promised that 'we shall try to arrange for riders' clothing to be washed at [after] each stage'. The reserves listed on the programme were made-up names to make the race look good. Two Frenchmen who travelled all the way from Atherstone to Wolverhampton in the back of a van were allowed to ride again next day, but not before being abandoned at their accommodation and having to join the race 30 minutes late.

It's easy to chuckle at the things that went wrong, the distances sometimes quoted as 'approximate' because the race took so much longer than expected – more than five hours for the 'approximately 103 miles' of stage four, more than seven and a half hours for 149 miles on stage five, for instance – and tales of officials and reporters being left behind. The truth is that, as Messenger says, nobody knew what he was doing: 'The officials were inexperienced and their resources were being taxed to the limit. By stage four, the few still around had sunken cheeks and hollow eyes and still had two stages to complete.' Considering all that, the race turned out to be a triumph. It had all but bankrupted the BLRC, which still owed prize money long afterwards, and it swallowed all but 1s 9d of the £100 1s 9d that Jimmy Kain had in his savings. But Britain now had a race which put it on the same stage as the Tour de France ... although somewhat closer to the wings than the spotlight, of course. The result was:

Stage 1: Brighton – Putney Heath (52 miles)
        Ernie Clements,Wrekin CC
Stage 2: Potter's Bar – Wolverhampton (130 miles)
        Geoff Clark, Bradford CC
Stage 3: Wolverhampton – Bradford (98 miles)
        Alex Hendry, Glasgow Wheelers
Stage 4: Bradford – Newcastle (approx 103 miles)
        Charles van Lerberghe, France
Stage 5: Newcastle – Glasgow (149 miles)
        Robert Batot, France

Overall:

1: Robert Batot	France	25:22:57
2: Geoff Clark	Bradford	25:28:41
3: Dennis Jaggard	London	25:29:18
4: Charles van Lerberghe	France	25:32:14
5: Jean Lauck	France	25:33:42
6: Marcel Waterschoet	France	25:41:23
7: George Edwards	Glasgow	25:41:23
8: Henry Nelc	France	25:43:26
9: Robert Poussel	France	25:46:05
10: Jack Taylor	Teesside	25:54:00

The number of Frenchmen in the top ten is what strikes immediately: the winner plus four others. Add the team award and first three in the mountains and you wonder not only how inexperienced the British riders must have been but just who these athletic foreigners were. The one thing you can be sure is that they weren't an official French team. The BLRC wasn't Britain's international body and the UCI would deal only with the NCU – with whom, after all, it had been dealing since the start. There are dissidents and nonconformists everywhere, France included, so the BLRC went through Soho café owners called Victor and Margot Berlemont to contact a communist sports organisation, the Fédération Sportive et Gymnastique du Travail.

Communists had become a force in France through their work in the Resistance. They collected more votes and seats than any other party in the elections of 1945 and only a combination of other parties stopped their taking control. America was so worried at the red advance that plans were drawn up – although quickly abandoned – to invade. The communist preference for working outside the system, though, meant that the FSGT was followed by other dissident organisations elsewhere, and so the BLRC could operate, after a fashion, outside the UCI.

And the semi-professionals? A big subject. More in a moment.

8

WELCOME TO THE PLEASUREDROME

All things have their fashion. Canals, railways and internet shares, they have their day, make money for a few and lose plenty for many more. It's funny to think, when you look at the state of outdoor tracks now, that people thought they would be the pleasuredromes of an epoch. They were exciting places once and not just wind-cracked acres ridden by bored school kids in the afternoon and local roadmen on Tuesday nights.

If you look through the A-to-Z of London you can still make out where one of the most exciting dreams ended in tears and financial disaster. The road you're looking for is in Catford, which at the time was not a southern suburb but an outlying village. The street, just east of Catford and Catford Bridge stations, is Sportsbank Road. It's called that because it was there that spectators stood when they couldn't get a seat.

Catford track was said to be the first in the world with bankings. Its surface was smooth concrete, just right for the new pump-up tyres the lads had started to use. It was the dream of a bunch of teenagers led by a C. P. Sisley whose club in Catford in April 1886 went so well that it had branches in Bristol, Cardiff, Nottingham and even Paris. The Catford members held races through the village and thousands of people turned up. The riders had clever heads as well as fast legs and they began to think of the money they could raise if they could charge those spectators for watching. They couldn't do it on the road, so they built a track instead, with seats for 1,000.

Time and again those seats would fill and late-comers would have to stand on the earth bank in what is now Sportsbank Road. Wonderful international matches were held there featuring riders like Jimmy Michael, the 5-foot Welshman who was Britain's first World Champion, winning the 1895 100-kilometre motor-paced title four kilometres ahead of Rik Luyten of Belgium. Michael looked like a 15-year-old, a 'childlike face topped a body lightly sloped forwards and always motionless; only his legs moved and turned madly at the greatest speeds,' said one report. Michael dominated paced racing from 1895 to 1899 and made a fortune.

The biggest event at Catford was the Chain Race, in which rival chain-makers employed riders to show their own ideas were best.

Harry Carrington has been a member of the Catford for almost 60 years and has written its history. He was 92 when I spoke to him and he apologised for 'not getting out cycling much these days'.

The chain companies paid untold sums to prove their point. It defeated the whole purpose because money bought you pacing teams and those who bought the best pacer won the race. The Simpson people brought over the Gladiator pacers from Paris and they were just that much better than the Dunlop team and so Simpson won the match. But who's heard of Simpson and his invention now?

It was a superb meeting, with American stars arriving on the liner from New York, and the appearance of the ill-fated Bordeaux–Paris winner, Arthur Linton. Catford should have become a track as famous as the Vigorelli in the 1960s and Bordeaux in the 1990s. It was one of the world's most glamorous venues. Sadly, it lasted just five years, from 1895 to 1900, and its losses all but crippled the club. Carrington said:

A syndicate opened the Herne Hill track about the same time [1891] and then the Crystal Palace track was rebuilt [opening in 1897]. The Boer War was on, there was general poverty, men were away in the army. There was too much competition for three tracks within a few miles of each other. And they leased the land with the condition, I suppose, that they returned it in the condition they got it in. So not only did building the track cost a fortune but running it lost another one and then demolishing it afterwards brought the club to its knees. It was generally a disaster.

Other new tracks opened, too, among them The Butts in Coventry in 1881, and Fallowfield in Manchester in 1892. Exeter – where the Empire Championships were held in 1910 – opened in 1894 and the disastrous World Championship track at New Brighton opened in 1898. Canning Town in London opened in 1897, and White City, also in London, opened in time for the Olympic Games in 1908.

Typically they were four laps to a mile, although Herne Hill was 550 yards, Portsmouth 586, and White City an enormous 640 ('when the wind blew over from Wormwood Scrubs, the going was particularly hard,' said the British World Sprint Champion, Bill Bailey). The size betrays the way cycling emerged from the culture of athletics. Running tracks were four laps or fewer to a mile, and so were bike tracks because cyclists originally rode on the cinders on which the runners competed, and the same officials ran both.

Crystal Palace, home of the glass exhibition hall for the 1851 Great Exhibition, was also the venue for the World Championships of 1908. Britain's hero was the Londoner Leon Meredith, born in February 1883 and usually known as Jack. In 1908 he won a gold medal from *Cycling* for becoming the first British rider to ride 100 miles out-and-home on the road at 20 mph. He started at 2.30 p.m. in Hounslow and rode what is now the A4, turning at the sixtieth milestone between Newbury and Hungerford.

Bidlake remembered seeing Meredith 'sail through the crowded, narrow street at Maidenhead at shoppers' teatime. He literally hand-assisted people out of his way, he edged through most marvellously, treating the road like a crowded track with an expert's skill in shooting through the tiniest gap, determined not to be bottled or shut in from his final sprint'. I love that 'hand-assisted'.

Meredith's Rover bike, with an 84-inch gear and 7-inch cranks, was put on show at the Gamages department store in central London. He said in 1903 that: 'I rise every morning at 5 a.m., because I am in the building contracting line, and one has to be out and about early. I ride seven or eight miles before a breakfast of good old porridge followed by either steak, chops, fish or eggs, washed down with tea.'

He then rode a few laps of Paddington track before cycling to the building site, he said, followed by another 20 or 30 miles at midday and another bash round the track in the evening 'taking lap-and-lap with all-comers and a fast five miles on my own now and again'.

His uncle, William Boyer, ran a building business from a canal wharf in Paddington. Meredith worked for him and rode his bike from one building site to the next. Mike Price of the *Independent*, in his history of the Olympics, says: 'His uncle's contracting business meant that Meredith was able to have a full-time trainer, a pacing machine, a masseur, the best facilities, and he could travel throughout Europe racing against top competition.' By contrast, Dave Marsh, the World Road Champion in 1922, remembered earning £1.50 a week and spending £1 a time for a tubular.

Meredith won the motor-paced championship at Crystal Palace despite crashing and using a succession of motorbikes to pace him. The four were 'coming on and off the track just as in a tandem-paced race [because] the engines soon became overheated,' said Bill Bailey. Meredith reckoned he switched pacers twenty times.

Bad luck dogged him. Rain fell throughout the Olympic Games in 1908 and Meredith crashed repeatedly on the slippery bankings of the new track at White City, London. It fell so much that the track was often under water and no medals were awarded for the sprint because the weather made the final run over its time limit. Tickets were cut from a shilling to sixpence and many spectators couldn't see the racing for umbrellas. Had it not been for all that, Meredith could have won more than just the team pursuit medal.

By then, though, it hardly mattered. Britain had five of the six golds: Tom 'Tiny' Johnson (whose ashes were scattered at Herne Hill in 1966) in the one-lap time-trial; Ben Jones in the 5-kilometre; Charlie Kingsbury in the 20-kilometre; Meredith, Jones, Kingsbury and Ernie Payne (who played football for what became Manchester United) in the team pursuit; and Charles Bartlett in the 100-kilometre track-race held instead of a road-race. And Meredith himself also won the World Motor-Paced Championship seven times between 1904 and 1913.

He learned from his uncle and became a rich man, so rich that the British Olympic Association told the NCU to give him no expenses for going to the ill-fated Olympic time-trial at Lake Malar.

Mike Price says: 'He acquired the rights to the Hubbard patent for a type of racing tyre and set up the Constrictor Tyre Company in Nursery Lane, Forest Gate [north-east London]. He had already built a roller-skating rink in Cricklewood Broadway, and he showed that it was more than a business interest when he became Britain's five-mile skating champion.'

The former World Champion Bill Bailey, Meredith's friend, filled in the detail:

In the early days of cycling there were cycling academies, where cycling was taught, like a motor-driving school but indoors, and a relative of Jack's ran one at the Porchester Hall, off Queensway, London. When interest dropped off, this relative asked Mrs Meredith to take it over for her son, Jack. She did – and just at that time the roller-skating boom started. Jack was ready for it, and never looked back.

He could not take money fast enough. Later, in partnership with Bill Skuse, who used to be one of his pacemakers, he built and opened another rink at Cricklewood. One night, when ambling round the Porchester Hall rink, Jack came up alongside and said 'Bill, I've just bought a tyre company for a hundred quid.' I nearly fell on my back. It appeared that Jack had a skating instructor by the name of Bain, whose brother was with the Constrictor Tyre Company, and Meredith was approached for financial assistance.

Before long, Jack was installed as Managing Director in place of Mr Hubbard, the inventor of the original Constrictor tyre, and Joe Bain remained in charge of production.

Old-timers speak of Constrictor as a great *marque* of the British bike industry. Its tubulars weren't sewn at the base, with all that meant for tricky mending of punctures. Instead, the tube was accessible through two sets of threads crossing each other diagonally without being stuck together. As well as being easier to repair, the stitching meant the tyre was less likely to fail suddenly. Bill Bailey said: 'I used to insist on a Constrictor tubular on the front. It might puncture, but I knew it would never burst. And that was important when doing a last 200 metres of 10.8 seconds!'

Meredith began importing Bastide bikes from France and wanted to fit them with equipment from BSA. The hubs came with small flanges, which didn't suit Meredith, who wanted more rigid wheels. He ordered 1,000 modified hubs from BSA and insisted, because of the size of the order, that they were stamped 'Constrictor'. It was an early example of marketing which would be imitated after the second world war by the racer and importer Ron Kitching.

Mike Price says: 'Meredith was recognised as the pioneer of lightweight racing fittings in Britain.' He stayed in the sport when he retired and picked World Championship road teams for the NCU, a tricky job when most riders knew only time-trials and track racing. He died of a heart attack on 29 January 1930, a week before his 48th birthday, while walking in Switzerland. He was buried in Willesden cemetery under wreaths sent by cyclists from all over Europe. His widow gave one of his trophies to the National Cyclists Union for a season-long competition.

The medals that Meredith and others won in 1908 were the last individual golds that Britain won in the Olympics for more than 80 years, until Chris Boardman in 1992. Harry Ryan and Thomas Lance won the now abandoned tandem sprint at Antwerp in 1920 but they, of course, won as a team.

On the other hand, no track championship has been as good for Britain as 1954 at Cologne. Britain won both the professional and amateur sprint – Reg Harris and a south London glass-blower called Cyril Peacock respectively; Pete Brotherton came second and Norman Sheil third in the amateur pursuit; and Joe Bunker won the bronze in the professional motor-paced.

For Reginald Hargreaves Harris – the 'Reg' in 'Reg rides a Raleigh' – it was the last gold medal. He was a hero of *Eagle* and *Boy's Own Paper*. He even came back in his mid-50s and won the British professional title. The only thing he couldn't organise was his business life.

I met him a couple of years before he died, in a hideaway cottage at Lower Withington in Cheshire, a silver-haired man given to cravats and chatting with blazer-wearing buffers in the pub. 'I rode races with only a single-minded outlook,' he said as we walked by the stables in the cottage grounds, 'and that was to win. And I didn't take it very well when I was beaten.'

He didn't take well to criticism, either. Shortly before seeing him, I'd visited his old rival, Jan Derksen, in his house under the flight path for Amsterdam airport. Derksen had told me Harris was a bomb: he'd explode and it was awful for everyone close by, but that after that there was nothing left. I repeated the story in *Cycling* and Harris did two things: the first was that he hit the roof; the second was that he was so angry that, thankfully, he hadn't noticed who'd written it. This, after all, was the man who flung tea over a reporter who'd asked how much he had been paid to lose a World Championship (a legendary story, this, and not typical of Harris's dealings with the Press; he sat for many hours with a youthful Jock Wadley, later the doyen of cycling journalists, without once asking who he was or why he was asking so many questions).

Little in Harris's story is less than extraordinary. He was nearly burned alive in a tank in the North African desert during the war, for instance. His injuries were so bad that he was discharged from the army and sent home. He won the World Amateur Sprint in 1947, then came close to being thrown out of the Olympic Games in London the following year because he left the training camp at Herne Hill without permission to train at Fallowfield (a Manchester track he would later own and rename the Reg Harris Stadium). 'I have never understood why people who have never interfered with my training methods or questioned my judgement should do so now,' he said of the NCU. He said he would take his case to the Games chairman, Lord Burghley. Then the bike trade said it wouldn't pay half the £800 it had promised the NCU for its training camp if Harris wasn't allowed to train as he chose, and that settled the matter.

What would now make a fairy story is if Harris had won despite it all. In fact he was outwitted by a 20-year-old Italian student called Mario Ghella and had to settle for silver. Hundreds had queued outside Herne Hill to see them ride. Harris also took silver in the tandem sprint with Alan Bannister. The official report says: 'The final of the tandems, saw, perhaps the most thrilling of the cycling events, and it was all the more to be regretted, therefore, that the darkness made it so difficult to follow.' Tommy Godwin took bronze in the kilometre; and Geldard, Godwin, Ricketts and Waters bronze in the team pursuit behind France and Italy.

The London Games were put on amid the damage of war and in such rationing that sympathetic nations sent food, and overseas riders brought extra rations. Eddie Wingrave, when he worked as a whip at Herne Hill, remembers he had to pay for his own uniform. It came to more than the price of tickets in the best seats every night. In other words he paid more to work than he would have done to spectate.

Such was the shortage of everything, including transport and fuel, that teams were expected to ride to the road-race circuit at Windsor. The official report records: 'In fact, nothing like this happened... nearly all the competitors [insisted] that the cycles should be conveyed to and from the training grounds on every occasion. Operators refused to take the machines aboard with their owners for fear of damage to the seats of the coaches, so lorries and furniture vans were brought into service. This brought complaints from some teams that they were prevented from accompanying their bicycles.' The report adds that 'an eight-seater vehicle was badly damaged in Windsor Park when an excited cycle coach attempted to drive the vehicle away. Two buses, one in London and one in Henley, were driven away by competitors'.

Television coverage was good but hardly anybody saw it. There were only 80,000 sets in the whole country and most broadcasts didn't reach more than 50 miles. A man did write in from the Channel Islands, though, to say he'd watched odd bits when the clouds cleared.

Harris then let slip that he planned to turn professional. That in those days, he said, was all it took. The idea became the fact and the NCU declared him from then on to be a professional. If the word suggested he was making much money at it, he wasn't. He still worked by day and trained at evenings and at weekends, riding a track bike on the roads around where Jodrell Bank now stands. It was ironic for a man who saw little risk in training on a bike with no brakes that he should be rammed in his sports car as he headed for the 1948 Good Friday Herne Hill meeting in London. Harris was busted up like an old banjo. His back was broken, his legs paralysed and the medical service swore he'd never walk again, let alone ride a bike. Just months later he became Professional

Champion of the World. If it wasn't true, you wouldn't dare write it.

The man that Harris out-rode in Copenhagen was Jan Derksen, who upset him all those years later. It wasn't Derksen who provided Harris's most colourful opposition, though. That came from another Dutchman, a puritanical-looking man called Arie van Vliet. He came from a richer background than Harris, from a family that ran a garage business, and he didn't ride a bike until his brother persuaded him. The next year he was Olympic Kilometre Champion. The two made a good living out of their rivalry. Harris identified van Vliet's weakness as 'never having been out in a cape and sou'wester and ridden in the rain for eight hours'.

Harris rode for Raleigh and dominated World Championships so much that, he insisted, the UCI changed the rules and made the sprint finals three-man rather than two-man races in an effort to stop him.

In 1958 the world championships were in Paris. Harris was riding and so was a lad called Cyril Bardsley, who was one of the other two in van Vliet's heat. Recognising that Bardsley was a no-hoper, the Dutchman asked Harris to make an arrangement. 'He could maybe lead me out in the sprint,' he suggested. Harris not only declined but explained van Vliet's weaknesses to Bardsley. 'The heat was being run,' Harris said, 'and Bardsley got himself shut in. Van Vliet was in third position and knew he couldn't stay there. And he shut down on Bardsley, who collected two or three broken spokes in his front wheel.'

Bardsley was new to World Championships and not sure of officialdom. Harris told him to protest. 'I said, "Show your wheel to the chief judge and make a case that it was before the 200-metre mark." It was just about on it, but it could have been two or three metres before it or after it.' The officials, in fact, backed van Vliet. But the Dutchman was hopping mad and blamed Harris. A long personal and professional friendship was about to end. And van Vliet was to extract his revenge.

Towards the end of the series, Harris, van Vliet and the Swiss rider, Oskar Plattner, were up together. It was a championship that Harris was not to win. 'I got fixed up,' he said. 'Plattner [the other riders called him "Corporal" because of his bossy ways] drew number one and crawled away from the start at the bottom of the track. Van Vliet moved into second place, going even slower, and Plattner was opening up a gap because of van Vliet, which put me close to van Vliet's back wheel. And so close to his wheel that I couldn't move round van Vliet to move into second position.'

Then Plattner put his head down and took off. I couldn't go around van Vliet because I was too slow. The moment I moved round him, I would have slipped over because of the 45-degree banking. By the time we got to the end of the first banking and I *could* get away from him, Plattner was probably 40 yards ahead and going for the lick of his life. And so I did the only thing I could do, which was chase, and I chased for half a lap and swung out for van Vliet to come past and continue, if only for the public. But he swung out with me and I knew then that I was fixed up.

There were four in the repechage. Van Vliet went first, Harris counter-attacked and van Vliet shut down on him. 'So we had a shoving match then. We were leaning on each other the whole length of the back straight.' In all that kerfuffle, neither qualified, and both had to sit and watch the final in what can only be described as a bad mood.

The following Thursday, there was the enormous revenge match that always took place in Amsterdam, with 50,000 spectators. Normally I'd share a large dressing-room with van Vliet, but I went and got in with some of the other lads in their dressing-room. And I happened to see Arie in the riders' quarters and he said 'What's wrong with my dressing-room? Isn't it big enough tonight?' And I said, 'No, it never will be again for the two of us.'

Harris won that night, beating van Vliet by the length of the straight.

And that was the start of an enormous bloody war. Everywhere that van Vliet and I raced, we weren't friends. We were bitter enemies. I mean, even that night, my wife and I were staying at his home – previously arranged – and my wife was sitting with his wife and his two teenage sons were there and they were in tears – 'What's happened to daddy?' – you know – and we didn't have a friendly word. And every time Arie said, 'Look, isn't it time this was over?' I'd say, 'It'll never be over so far as I'm concerned.' It got that way that some of the other riders were saying, 'When are you two going to shake hands?' because life was getting bloody tough every time we were engaged anywhere. There was crossfire and other guys were getting caught in it.

In the end it just died out, after fifteen months. The two stayed in occasional touch.

The excitement they generated was the final flare of professional sprinting. Harris's was the last era when sprinters could dominate a programme. He won four Professional World Championships – 1949, 1950, 1951 and 1954 – and through the 1950s was the only cyclist that most outsiders had heard of. 'Who d'you think you are, Reg Harris?' was the way policemen pulled up kids they thought riding too fast on their bikes.

For all that sprinters pulled in crowds, few had sponsorship contracts as firm as Harris's. He rode throughout the height of his career for Raleigh, his bikes made in Nottingham by Bill Blackamore. It meant never having to ride six-days, never riding anything he didn't fancy. But what he fancied, and which I've never seen mentioned, could be surprising. Ken Joy, the road record-breaker, remembers a discussion in the bar at the London cycle show.

'It would have been 1952, 1953, that sort of time and Reg could see that his time on the track wouldn't last for ever,' Joy told me. 'And that was when British companies were putting money into road-racing, and there was money in it. He took me to one side and suggested we should start a road team together. His idea was that I would look after the dirty work in the bunch and he would win the sprints. I can't remember whether anybody else was involved but I know it never came to anything.'

As well it might not, this matching of Harris the sprinter who had probably never ridden more than ten consecutive miles at top level with Joy the time-triallist who dismissed his experiences in road-races as 'like glorified club runs, spending 75 per cent of your time on someone else's wheel'.

Unsatisfied as a road rider, more than content with his track record, Harris retired when he was 37, in 1957. In 1971 he was having dinner with Gerald O'Donovan, a director of Carlton Cycles and the man behind Raleigh's lightweight division. O'Donovan said Harris should ride the British Sprint Championship a few weeks later. Harris took it as a joke and laughed. He was 51 and keener on having a holiday in Scotland.

O'Donovan hadn't meant it as a joke, though, and he organised a bike and a ride. Harris, a grey-haired, patrician figure now, went to the Meadowbank track in Edinburgh and asked officials half his age if he could have a practice ride.

'Have you ridden on a track before?' someone asked. Harris promised that he had. 'But have you ever ridden on a proper track like this?' the official persisted, gesturing at the steep wooden bankings. Harris said that, yes, he had. Then someone asked who he was.

He got to the semi-final, where he faced Gordie Johnson, the Australian who'd won the world championship in 1970 but now held a British licence. Harris said:

Johnson was obviously fitter than me and he must have thought I was a pushover, as I would have done at his age. He took it easy in the back straight, but I still had a lively jump. I outmanoeuvred him and won the match. It was the best of three and he won the other two.

In 1974 the championships were at Leicester. I was able to win and the championship aroused tremendous interest and I had a lot of column inches. The British pros were dumb to let me in, although in fairness they had been riding road-races. It illustrated the gap between the pros in my time and then. It was a good thing that they didn't come across me when I was a real bike rider.

Reg Harris, after winning the British Championship at the age of 54

Raleigh had always promised Harris a job when he stopped racing. Its managing director, Sir Harold Bowden, had offered him a seat on the board in 1950. He took him into the company's oak-panelled boardroom, offered him a liqueur and pointed out the chair already reserved for him.

Harry Traynor, Raleigh's Press Officer at the time, wrote that Harris would have fitted in well. 'The Lancashire lad with a cotton mill and cloth cap background had acquired – through assiduous practice and diligent application – a veneer of culture and sophistication worthy of an aristocratic country squire. Almost any large commercial organisation would have benefited from his incisive mind and abounding energy – natural assets which more than compensated for his impatience with fools and his contempt for mediocrity.'

Raleigh repeated the offer at the end of 1957, when Harris finally retired. But it was no longer the main board. It was an almost shed-in-the-garden operation. Gerald O'Donovan says in his private papers:

Raleigh had lost the capability of making true race and sports bikes and set up a scheme to start a Reg Harris bicycle company, to do that thing. At the last moment before implementation they got cold feet and did a very surprising thing. The chairman and the managing director designate came to us [Carlton Cycles] in great secrecy, saying in effect that we had been making something of a name for ourselves as experts in the field.

The result was that Carlton rather than Harris got the lightweight contract, which made Harris bitter for the rest of his life, although not personally with Gerald O'Donovan. Nothing remained of the job that Harris said Raleigh had promised. Shortly afterwards Raleigh was taken over by its rival, Tube Investments (which had bought the British Cycle Corporation to protect its market for cycle tubing) and Harris's hopes were over.

O'Donovan's recollection is that: 'The Reg Harris scheme was dead but did not completely lie down. We did start to make some bikes under that brand, but before we got to market them, Reg walked out and started up on his own.'

Harry Traynor said: 'In what is perhaps described as a fit of high dudgeon, Mr Harris decided to set himself up as a manufacturer of top-end lightweight bicycles. In doing so, he ignored a simple truth, namely that very, very few small cycle builders ever enjoyed the standard of living he had become accustomed to as master of a fourteen-acre estate with a splendid house and a miniature lake.'

The company failed and Harris lost the house, the estate and his second wife, Dorothy. Reduced from World Champion to Once Champion, he started selling the Gannex cloth that the prime minister, Harold Wilson, had made famous through his raincoats. Other sales jobs followed – 'I have to admit that saying "My name is Reg Harris, could I see you?" still opens doors,' he told me. 'Maybe people are just surprised to see you're still alive.' Finally he retired for good.

Years after their last meeting, Harry Traynor found Harris's address and visited him in 1990. The two hadn't met for more than 25 years. Traynor arrived at the same wooden gate that I had found. He said:

Any doubts that I had about stopping at the wrong address vanished as soon as I spotted the immaculate red car. A 3.5-litre Alfa Romeo GT 6, of course. And beyond the gleaming Alfa, two horses poking their heads through the stable doors. Two ferocious-looking doberman stood sentry in the driveway, and sitting sphinx-like at the door of the early18th-century cottage, a green-eyed Abyssinian cat.

All this the property of the man who, after being rejected by a cycling manufacturing colossus which eventually would be absorbed by Americans, set himself up in a small business that was doomed to failure from the outset. Fail it did, but not the man who dominated the world of track cycling for more than a decade.

Harris died aged 72 on 22 June 1992. He had a heart attack while cycling the previous day, then another a few hours later. His wife Jennifer said he'd told her he'd 'only be an hour and then we'll have a pub lunch'. He died in hospital at 2.30 a.m. The flowers at St John the Evangelist church in Chelford, south of Manchester, included a blue pillow with the symbol of the heron's head of Raleigh's trade mark.

Club riders across Britain raised £60,000 to start a training scheme in his name for young riders at the Manchester track, where his statue stands at the end of the finish straight. Harris never rode the track, which is indoors, steeply banked and made of wood, but his failed business ventures included the city's outdoor, shallow and hard-surfaced Fallowfield track – now demolished – which he renamed the Reg Harris Stadium.

9

SIX-DAY WONDERS

Harris never fell out totally with Raleigh. Mike Breckon, who worked in the company's marketing department, recalled that: 'One of my regular jobs was to go out and see Reg and take him for lunch; many of the others thought he belonged to the past even if they recognised that we ought to keep him happy, but to me, the enthusiast, it was the best job I could have.'

Had Raleigh not paid Harris to carry its name, he'd have been forced to make ends meet by riding six-day races. Given Derksen's assessment that Harris had a single *krachtexplosie* – explosion of strength – and then nothing else to offer, it's hard to see that he'd have been convincing for a whole week. Had he wanted to, though, he could have walked into any six-day in Britain and demanded the highest price to start. And he'd have been given it. The trouble is that there were no consistent six-days and the only real series started in 1967, ten years after he retired. It was run at Wembley in north London, in what had previously been the Empire Pool.

The stadium stands on the site of the Empire Exhibition held in 1923. The football ground alongside was all that survived of what must have been a tremendous show and that in turn began to be pulled down as the twenty-first century started. The Australian Palace alongside the stadium was one of the largest attractions but it was pulled down when the exhibition closed and the Empire Pool – renamed Wembley Arena in the late 1970s – was built where it stood.

In 1934 the Canadian entrepreneur and former track star Willy Spencer used it to sell a British idea back to the British. Spencer, who had himself been born in Manchester, used the Empire Pool for the first series of six-day races since the Agricultural Hall. In between time the six-day idea had been exported to America and had transmuted into the Madison. Spencer was now selling it back to the British.

There were fifteen teams and he squeezed in as many home riders as he dared. But it was a gamble because they were as inexperienced at bunched racing on steep boards as they were at racing in bunches on the roads.

Frank Southall, who'd turned pro for record-breaking on the road, crashed early on and went to hospital. So too did the Manchester rider Syd Cozens, who'll return to the story of British bike-racing as manager of its first full professional team.

Southall had been paired with the much more experienced Torchy Peden of Canada and Cozens with the less experienced Harry Grant of Britain. Spencer tried to build the survivors into a new team for the rest of the race but it didn't work and both were given twelve hours to find new partners. Peden couldn't do it and dropped out. Grant was removed from the race two hours later.

Only nine of the original fifteen teams survived the six days. The winners were Gustav Kilian and Heiz Vopel of Germany with 1,938 miles, beating the Belgian pair of Albert Buysse and Jean Aerts. The series lasted until 1939, when the race was won by a 6ft 2in Belgian called Karel Kaers and his countryman Omer de Bruycker. Then came the war. The Empire Pool was used to house people evacuated from Gibraltar to escape the expected bombing and shelling as British troops tried to control access to the Mediterranean.

In America six-day racing struggled on between the wars, but the Depression and the stock market crash finished it off. That and changing tastes. Annual sixes in Boston ended in 1933, in Detroit in 1936, Chicago in 1948. New York, where it started, held on until 1950.

Races before the war were run by a Mr Big called John Chapman. Riders hated his emperor-like rule over their lives and wages but he kept the public coming in and the riders in wages. His successor, Harry Mendel, on the other hand, cut costs by signing lots of German riders but not always the biggest. The strongest of them were Kilian and Vopel. They were worthy riders but Chapman wouldn't spend out on decent opposition and crowds started staying away when Kilian and Vopel won twelve races in a row, then another nine. Madison Square Garden, where the tag-race six-day idea had started, no longer saw the race as a bankable proposition and moved it from its regular date in December and put on the skater Sonja Henie instead.

The coffin was nailed but the ghost still walked. Jimmy 'The Whale' Proscia had a go in New York, Chicago, Montreal and other cities and even attracted the 1951 Tour winner, Hugo Koblet. But the money wasn't there. The track was portable and thin. A crash could push a pedal through the surface. Crowds stayed away. It was a sad end.

So why, then, should the six-day idea come back to London in 1967? The answer comes in the juxtaposition of a desperate Dutchman and a struggling national bike show. No one who went to Earl's Court in 1967 will forget the booming voice of the organiser, Charles Ruys, announcing: *'Tien pond voor de eerste ronde.'* You could hear it imitated in bike shops all over the land. It seemed a fortune but our belief that professional bike racers would get excited about winning £10 for taking a lap just showed the happy naïvete of those of us in the crowd who emptied our pockets to provide it. That we should raise no more than £10 a throw is quite something as well. We were so happy that we never questioned why we should be asked to pay to watch the race and then pay again to provide the prizes.

Ruys was a colourful character whose command of English meant he could outswear a tugboat captain. He started racing in Holland against his parents' wishes when he was 13. He insisted he'd tell his family he was staying with a friend and the friend would say he was staying with Charlie. Instead they went all over Holland, Belgium and northern France. The secret got out when Charlie's parents read in a newspaper that their son and his friend had won a Madison at Arnhem, though as with all Ruys' stories, there may be a degree of added colour.

Ruys and his wife went to Australia after the war and then to New Guinea, to get the money they needed to go back to Europe. The Australians, who ran New Guinea at the time, wouldn't give a bar licence to a Dutchman so he changed nationality. Being Australian got him into Britain in the days when there was no European Union and therefore fewer rights for a Dutchman to live there. It was as an Australian that he came to England in 1964, having left the promotions company that was just about to come up with the Amstel Gold Race.

Bluff and bluster, all part of the Ruys story, counted for little in a country where he was unknown, and life went wrong. He had to cash in his Dutch life insurance to live. Looking for work, he visited the annual cycle show at Earl's Court. He pronounced it dull and came up with the idea of a six-day race to liven it up. Except that he didn't. That was just his version of the story. In fact, the idea came from a London printer and cyclist called Keith Robins who, visiting the Motor Show for tips on how to perk up the 'dull' bike exhibition, told David Cooper of the bike and motorbike trade association that his advice was to build a track and run a six-day.

'David didn't know what a six-day or even an indoor track was,' says Robins. 'But he was interested and I got a call to go to Champion Spark Plugs with a budget. Charlie Ruys only came along and asked to be organiser once we'd got the thing running.'

Champion, on behalf of the trade, was the secondary sponsor, after the lager company, Skol. It made a historical loop because the founder, Albert Champion, had been a French cycling champion at the end of the nineteenth century. With panache, he then dropped dead at a dinner in his honour in 1927. The automobile industry was at the Hôtel Meurice in Paris to honour him for making the spark plugs that got the solo flyer Charles Lindbergh across the Atlantic that same year, when he keeled over at their feet after a heart attack. 'It made for a classy final scene,' says Peter Nye, the American writer working on Champion's biography.

Two things happened after that meeting with the company that shared Champion's name. The first was that Ruys asked to run the London six in 1967 and was given the job and the second was that in 1968 he borrowed the track to take to Holland. There he covered it with Dutch advertising. Robins says: 'He brought it back to London with the adverts obliterated by plastic emulsion but on the afternoon before the show we found that none of the riders could stay upright on it. We had to spend hours scrubbing the paint so they could ride. Skol were so fed up with the trouble and the expense that Ruys wasn't asked back.'

The 1967 and 1968 events were run on a knockabout track 152 metres round, built not of smooth planks laid parallel and staggered but on 144 sheets of plywood nailed to a frame. It kept the cost to a bargain £30,000. If you remember threepenny coins with their angled edges and rounded corners, taking the 50-degree bankings would have been like riding round the inside of one of them. It was a long and thin track, like a cigar, perfect for madison-racing but useless for paced races – not that that stopped the naïve crowd cheering delightedly at the Derny races.

TICKET APPLICATION FORM

The 1967 race started each day at 10 a.m. and went on to 11 p.m., with breaks for lunch and tea, like a cricket match. British fans, never quick to part with their money, wouldn't spend 50p on tickets for the first session and officials had to give out tickets to anyone who'd come in for nothing so Angus Ogilvy would have something to open, or at least a crowd to see him do it.

The winners weren't Peter Post and Gerard Koel as predicted – and as many people now remember it – but the Danes Palle Lykke and Freddy Eugen. Post, the era's most prolific six-day winner, had become the race's main attraction following the death of Tom Simpson – who'd also contracted to ride – three months earlier in the Tour de France. Years later I visited Post at his home in Amstelveen and we sat in a main room that had that same decor you find in every Novotel and Holiday Inn, all neutral creams with contrasting patches of something warmer. It maybe demonstrated the kind of life he'd lived for decades, always moving, always staying in faultless but bland hotels. The one personal touch was a huge coloured picture of a motocross rider.

At first Post started eulogising London as a place that every rider dreamed to be, the very capital of the world. Then I gave him a metaphorical kick on the shins and he stopped and smiled ruefully and said: 'Yes, we had a few problems that year. That was Charles Ruys that year, wasn't it? There wasn't so much money and the organisation didn't quite come together.'

I asked him about the rumour that all the visiting Continentals had been asked to ride on limited gears to avoid drubbing the home professionals, talented but out-of-their-depth lads like Dave Bonner and Bill Lawrie. He smiled and looked at the shoes at the end of his stretched-out legs and said: 'We had to limit the gears, I know. The English, *ja* ... they were a bit ... but soon we could see that it was going to be all right.'

This, incidentally, was franker than his immediate post-race comment in *Cycling* that 'for a first time, the organisation of your six was really fantastic'. Or maybe it depended on the weight you placed on 'for a first time'.

Cycling wrote of the last hour:

One continuous cheer now, the crowd was powerless to do anything but cheer, stamp feet, draw breath, and cheer again. For imperceptibly the Danes were gaining. Then suddenly they had made it – the last 20 yards were gained in no time, with Freddy Eugen latching on the back – four minutes it had taken them to gain the lap, four minutes which meant victory over six days.

The editor, Alan Gayfer, wrote: 'To come out of a six-day race into the midnight air is like taking a cold shower, both physically and mentally.'

Ruys started his follow-up for 1968. But the bike trade could no longer afford Earl's Court and its cycle exhibition moved to Manchester. There was nowhere big enough there for a track, and the trade, which had heavily subsidised London, couldn't afford a second race. Skol stayed as sponsor and the venue moved to Wembley, where the track reappeared from Holland with its painted-out Dutch advertising. A year later Ron Webb, another Australian who had looked after the British riders under Ruys, took over as organiser.

Webb arranged another track, also portable. The original was dismantled and stored for a while to try to justify the hopes of the sports minister, Denis Howell, that it would find 'a permanent and useful home'. A Midlands organisation was said to want it as part of a sports centre. It never happened. The track stands now in an aircraft hangar alongside the Solent at Calshot, operated by Hampshire County Council for school-kids and anyone else who wants to book it. It was made shorter than ever to get it into its new home and it has never again been used for proper racing.

Ruys returned to Holland to get what work he could find. The Amstel Gold Race, the Classic he had dreamed of running, had been announced in 1966 and there was no way back for Ruys into the team that started it. He took to writing rambling articles for *Sporting Cyclist* and *Cycling*, helped Graham Webb get established in Holland and win the 1967 World Road-Race Championship – that story will turn up later, remember – then dropped from the picture. I last saw him in 1983 by the little outdoor track in Oudenbosch, a Dutch village near the Belgian border. He was the same shape, big but even rounder, the face older and weary. He was far less ebullient now, reduced to running the equivalent of Coventry track league. I wanted to talk to him but, frankly, I couldn't think of anything to say. He died a few years later.

Bryan Wotton's estimation is that he was 'just another man with a foreign accent who entranced British cycling'.

Bike shows in Britain had a troubled history after Earl's Court and never again was a six-day run in conjunction with one. There were a handful of trade stands around the track at Wembley but that was all. Ron Webb, seeing how Ruys had been unable to persuade British cyclists to watch in the afternoon, ran his race only in the evenings, from 7 p.m. until midnight. He called it not a six-day but a six. The distinction was the result of a row with Continental organisers who thought his race half-weight, which of course it was. By 1974–1975, though, they too had all abandoned most afternoon racing, just as one by one they had given up keeping their stadiums open all night. Far from being a literal six-day, events now have a minimum total duration of just *one* day: 24 hours.

The difference is that most of the Continental events continue. Webb's wonder died when Allied Breweries, owner of the Skol brand, ended its sponsorship after 1980. Hopes of moving elsewhere were killed by the cost of venues. It wasn't that Webb couldn't sell seats; it was that so many seats would have to be taken out of a stadium to accommodate the track that there was too little left in ticket money to pay the rent. The portable track saved one set of expenses but introduced another, because the venue had to be paid for while the track was built and then demolished.

It's the problem that the race promoter Alan Rushton faces now. Britain's biggest organiser would love to put on a six-day but Manchester, the only track that could accommodate it, has too few seats to make it pay.

The first and only Briton to win a London six-day since the war was the Londoner Tony Gowland, a red-haired and freckled man with a round face who had the reputation of a tough sprinter. He was helped in 1972 by being paired with the even faster Patrick Sercu of Belgium, a rider who startled the field as an unknown youngster at Herne Hill some years earlier by simply riding away from everyone. The one British rider to make a consistent career of the six-day, though, was Tony Doyle, who began in the London six of 1980. By the time a crash ended his career, he had won 23 events. Doyle was an early talent, showing well in junior road-races and by the age of 21 in 1980 rode the Olympic Games in Moscow. He rode the team pursuit, but Britain's hopes ended in the quarter-final. He came back to Britain disillusioned and turned professional in August that same year, in time to ride the National Championship Pursuit at Leicester. He trained for 1,200 miles in the two previous weeks and won the gold medal. A month later he won the World Professional Pursuit in Besançon, despite being bitten by a police dog the previous day. That brought him a contract to partner Udo Hempel in the London six-day, his first, which he finished eighth.

In 1983 he won his first event, with Danny Clark. It was with the Tasmanian that Doyle shared 19 of his 23 six-day victories, a partnership record shared only by Rik van Steenbergen and Émile Severeyns and by Peter Post and Fritz Pfenninger.

Then on the fourth night of the Milan six in November 1989 he crashed into Marat Ganeev as the Russian swung up the banking. Doyle lay unconscious at the foot of the track with brain damage, a broken right shoulder and a lung injury. For a while there were those who doubted he would live. Yet Doyle not only raced again but returned to Munich, once more with Clark, and won.

By then the pair had won too often and promoters refused to let them make a pairing. Doyle raced until he was 37, retiring after damaging his spine in a crash at Zurich in November 1994. But that wasn't the end of the story. In December 1995 he was elected president of the British Cycling Federation, dislodging Ian Emmerson, a long-serving official and race promoter. Among those who expressed surprise was the head of the Union Cycliste Internationale, of which Emmerson was vice-president.

Emmerson, a race official and promoter from near Lincoln, had been a hands-on, administrative president. Doyle by contrast wanted to be a figure-head. He found favour with BCF members who believed the federation had grown stale and too much dominated by the admittedly vague concept of 'men in blazers'. Riders saw Doyle as their man – even though he had already insisted that he wanted to be no more than a figure-head – whereas those already trying to make things happen kept confidence in Emmerson.

The row between both parties became acrid. The allegations and counter-allegations were so complex and legally dangerous that *Cycling* had to stop reporting them. The sorry business came to an embarrassing and expensive end on 19 February 1997, when the BCF's technical director, Colin Clews, apologised in the High Court and paid Doyle damages for claiming on BCF notepaper that Doyle had been dishonest, had hidden commercial relationships which influenced his actions as BCF president to the detriment of the BCF and its members, and in particular that Doyle had 'shown utter contempt for the views of the majority; for the faith put in him by the membership'.

The damages and a whole-page legal statement in *Cycling* ended one of the most extraordinary and costly blunders a BCF officer had ever made.

THE SIXES OF LONDON

1923   Alois Persyn (B) – Pierre Vandevelde (B)
1934   Piet van Kempen (B) – Syd Cozens (GB)
1936   Gustav Kilian (G) – Heinz Vopel (G)
1937   Piet van Kempen (B) – Albert Buysse (B)
1938   Albert Buysse (B) – Albert Billiet (B)
1939   Karel Kaers (B) – Omer De Bruycker (B)
1951   Albert Bruylandt (B) – René Adriaensens (B)
1952   Alf Strom (Aus) – Reg Arnold (Aus)
1967   Palle Lykke (Den) – Freddy Eugen (Den)
1968   Patrick Sercu (B) – Peter Post (H)
1969   Patrick Sercu (B) – Peter Post (H)
1970   Patrick Sercu (B) – Peter Post (H)
1971   Patrick Sercu (B) – Peter Post (H)
1972   Patrick Sercu (B) – Tony Gowland (GB)
1973   Gerben Karstens (H) – Leo Duyndam (H)
1974   Patrick Sercu (B) – René Pijnen (H)
1975   René Pijnen (H) – Gunther Haritz (G)
1977   Patrick Sercu (B) – René Pijnen (H)
1978   Don Allan (Aus) – Danny Clark (Aus)
1979   Patrick Sercu (B) – Albert Fritz (WG)
1980   Don Allan (Aus) – Danny Clark (Aus)

10

THE NAME ON THE FRAME

Doyle and a hundred thousand other riders thought nothing of professionals saying who had made their bikes, sometimes even urging others to buy from the same factory. That, after all, was the way they saw professionalism and sponsorship. It was their job to sell whatever their backers produced.

The idea of cashing in on your name is as old as cycling itself, and as poorly thought of in Britain for almost as long. Arthur Zimmerman, the 5ft. 11in. American world sprint champion with a taste for cigars, good living and late nights, accepted two bikes and possibly under-the-table payments from Raleigh, in whose advertisements he also appeared. In 1893 he took a liner to England where, says the writer Peter Nye, he was greeted enthusiastically by everybody but British officials, who banned him from racing in England. That was a real problem in the days when it took a week for an American to get back home. He went off and raced in Ireland and France, countries happy to pay no notice of what happened across the water.

Nye says:

> Professionalism was seen as a threat to the purity of the sport, something cycling officials vigilantly policed by expelling any amateurs who took advantage of their sport. Any rider branded a professional was effectively banished because amateur racing was where the action was.
>
> The English cycling officials' had no effect in America [where] League of American Wheelmen officials came to his defence and inquired into why their English counterparts suspended his racing. He remained eligible to compete in the premier world championships, open only to amateur men, at distances of one and ten miles.

The absurdity of Zimmerman's position was accentuated years later when the British rider Freddie Grubb turned up after his second place in the Olympics in Triumph's whole-page advertisements, in which the firm's name appeared an inch high and then, a fraction of the size, the acknowledgment 'F. H. Grubb, Rider'.

Rover took a page in *Cycling* in August 1908 to picture Charles Bartlett under the headline 'THE HERO OF THE OLYMPIC GAMES' and reprinted the *Daily Telegraph*'s report of his 100-km. victory. Montague A. Holbein, whose out-and-back '50' of 2:43:32 in 1889 beat the straight-out time and stood until pneumatic tyres appeared, used to endorse the quaintly named Anti-Stiff: 'Having been advised to try Anti-Stiff, I feel I have no hesitation in recommending its use after great exertion: it both soothes and strengthens the tired muscles...'

The expression for all these was 'maker's amateur'. Not quite a professional, but not strictly amateur. The French word was *indépendant*, which between the world wars became formalised into an intermediate category between amateur and professional. Independents could win money and wear advertising and they could ride against amateurs and professionals as they wished, although not both at the same time because amateurs were forbidden to ride with professionals.

Independents appeared in Brighton–Glasgow in 1946. The best, Geoff Hill of Hickman Cycles, finished no better than 11th, and cynics said that independents thereby justified their reputation of looking like professionals without the irritating need to be good enough to be one. Independents troubled the NCU and RTTC only because the BLRC allowed them to ride against amateurs. The RTTC saw no difference between an independent and a professional, the point being not the amount of money each received but that they received any money at all. To be paid to ride a bike gave them advantages over those who trained at night and raced at weekends as pure amateurs.

The RTTC chairman, Will Townsend, dismissed campaigns to let amateurs ride with independents as coming 'largely from those interested in the formation of a professional class of cycling'. In February 1957, he wrote:

There has been a great spate of propaganda, mainly for political reasons, seeking to persuade us that it is essential that amateurs and paid riders should compete with one another ... The argument runs that professionals and independents are superior riders (an argument which cannot always be accepted) and, therefore, if the amateur rides against the paid rider his performances will improve to such an extent that he will be able to win international events.

My comment on that is that, but for an accident within sight of the finish, Frank Southall and Harry Wyld would have won the world's road-race championship for Britain in 1925. They did not have to ride against professionals or independents to be so near success.

Townsend is a clever man. I knew him as chairman of my first racing club, the Westerley in west London. But his appeal against change was a shot in the foot. His motives were sincere – to protect 'the great mass of those who ride in cycling competition to "have a go"' – but to cite a race no less than 22 years earlier in which the British riders hadn't after all won suggested to opponents just how out of touch he and the RTTC were.

The NCU, which had dropped its ban on BLRC riders in 1953, stood firm against mixed-category racing until 1957. Then, surrendering to its members' wishes, it ended its agreement with the RTTC and allowed amateurs and independents to mix. Faced with being isolated if it stood firm, the RTTC agreed some weeks later not to ban amateurs who had raced against independents while still not allowing the two to race together under RTTC rules. The sport had, therefore, reached the absurd position where the RTTC was trying to keep quiet a sport which the commercial interests it had just acknowledged were trying to make as public as possible.

In fact, any fear that featherbedded independents would live a life of paid training and rest and rob the hardworking amateurs of races and prizes was ill-founded. Most had no more than a free jersey, sometimes a free bike but more usually a free frame, and always the promise of a bonus for winning. The fact that most never had a chance of winning made the bonus academic.

Dave Orford, who was an independent from 1946 to 1963, says what he calls 'the well-sponsored independent teams' – Viking (which began in 1948), BSA (1952), Dayton (1947) and Paris (1947) – 'had limited expenses and the use of a motor vehicle to reach events out of their area'.

This was the era when the UK still had a cycle industry, and so these teams were equipped with mainly British components, some of whom, like Cyclo Benelux, paid bonuses of £3 a win. As the money available was very small beer indeed, it was important for these small combines to race locally, so that if they didn't manage to win very often, they were not spending much in the way of expenses. Personally, I have ridden up to 40 miles to reach the start, contested an 80-mile race, then ridden home.

In fact, with the possible exception of win bonuses, the amateurs whose interests the RTTC defended often got more than the independents they considered unfairly favoured. Gerald O'Donovan of Carlton Cycles and later sponsor of the Raleigh professional team said: 'The world of club cycling was very well aware that the all-conquering Monckton Wheelers rode Carltons and it was rightly assumed that they had not paid for them. There were others; the lightweight cycle manufacturers waged an underground war in this area.'

Having dominated time-trialling, Carlton turned to track-racing, still with advertising as its motive. 'This brought Carlton its first World Championship and a host of national and international results, which did much to uphold the reputation [of Carlton],' said O'Donovan.

The UCI's idea, when it created independents, was that riders would try their hand against professionals to see if they were good enough to get a pro contract. It made sense in an era when a professional could never again race as an amateur. One false move would create both a failed professional and a doomed amateur.

The UCI wanted independents to take two years in which to decide whether to become a professional or go back to racing as an amateur. The problem in Britain was that the sport wasn't big enough for professionals. Nor, once a rider was an independent, would the governing bodies let him return as an amateur. Amateurs good enough to turn independent tended not to because amateurs got most of the selections for overseas races. Amateurs who did turn were, therefore, usually past their peak. And having become independent, there was no alternative but to keep on as one until age or boredom intervened. For all the talent in the British independent class, it was an elephants' graveyard.

That was the position that Derek Buttle, an east London rider whom everyone remembers as 'a real toughie' on his bike, was trying to resolve. He had turned not independent but fully professional for a series of races at Herne Hill track. When that faltered, he realised he had to save his career. There was little future on the track and so he took up a suggestion from John Dennis, the man running the Herne Hill fixtures, to approach Hercules Cycles.

The British bike industry was in its vainglorious years before extinction. Hercules was sponsoring record-breakers like Ken Joy and the rivalry between companies for the dwindling sales of the 1950s expanded into other extravagances which can only have hastened their collapse. Raleigh hired the Royal Albert Hall for its trade show; BSA rented the Park Lane Hotel in Mayfair; Hercules used the Piccadilly. No gesture was too much, too suicidal.

It was in that mood that 'Mac' McLachlan, the Hercules marketing executive, opened Derek Buttle's letter in 1952. And having read it, he dictated a letter on Hercules notepaper, which showed an address near where the M6 is now in Birmingham, near Fort Dunlop, and told Buttle he wanted to take it further.

What Buttle had suggested was a full professional road team to ride the Tour de France.

He laughed when I met him in the Suffolk house where he and his wife Sheila ran the post office for 30 years. 'Funny, isn't it?' he said. 'Britain had never had a proper professional team and now whether we got one depended on whether I could think of a hotel. I was just a bike rider. When he asked where we could meet, all I could think of were cafés. That's all I ever went to. You couldn't take a businessman to a café, could you?'

When Buttle joined a cycling club he was sure they'd do 100 miles every Sunday. 'I thought I'd get good enough and go out for 100 miles, and I rode it in about six hours, and I thought "That's easy!" So I did it again and I thought that if it was that easy, maybe I ought to try 200.'

He lived in east London, in East Ham. 'I rode off right round the Kent coast. And I took the biggest pasting I've ever had in my life. I felt awful. I don't know what time I got home but it was in the early hours of the morning.'

Undeterred, he joined the club at Cranham, which is where District Line trains are stored when they're not needed on the Underground. There he met a stumpy sprinter called Dave Bedwell and changed clubs. Bedwell came only waist-height and his frames were no bigger than key rings. He used to look at CTC rides and jeer 'You wouldn't see me dead with that lot.' The irony is that he died in 1999 on a CTC run in Devon.

Derek Buttle in the 1954 Tour of Britain

Bedwell and Buttle and riders formed the Dayton Cycles independent team with Len West and Les Scales. Their jerseys were blue and yellow and the advertisements for their bikes said 'All British' and 'supreme on Road and Track'. But being a professional would be better. Buttle turned professional – 'and to this day I don't know why I did' – to ride madisons at Herne Hill. He rode with Bedwell in a Claud Butler team – Butler was another London bike-maker – and remembers the difficulty of throwing in a rider only half his size. Buttle had turned pro for the track but didn't like it.

At his cottage in Suffolk he leaned back, trying to haul chunks of his life that went from his brain after a van mounted the pavement outside their house and hurled him unconscious into a tree in August 1992. Years of treatment have left him much better except that he wobbles when he gets out of the chair and there are gaps in his memory.

I remember I used to get on well with this chap at the NCU, because they were behind the Herne Hill races, and this chap said, 'Well, you may find Hercules are interested.' So I went to the library and I got out a book of all the companies in the country and I wrote to this chap McLachlan at Hercules. And to my surprise I got a reply to say he was interested and could we meet. That was when I was stuck. I couldn't think of anywhere. And then I remembered that the Tour of Britain had had a reception at a place called the Cora Hotel, which was near Euston station, so I suggested there.

Bryan Wotton remembers the Cora Hotel from committee meetings there. 'It was a hole,' he says.

McLachlan didn't seem put off. The two sat in a lounge, Buttle lean and young, McLachlan 'in his 50s, maybe, grey-haired, immaculate, very debonair, a gentleman. We sat there and we did the usual chatting and then he asked what I had in mind and it all happened as though he'd already made his mind up. He asked what we wanted and we settled on £500 a year plus bonuses'.

Remember that in 1952 a lot of Continental professionals didn't get paid at all. Buttle recalled: 'I met the footballer, Billy Wright, once. Remember him? He was at the top in those days. He asked what cyclists earned and I told him that with my bonuses I'd earned £851 that year and he looked impressed and said that was about what he was earning.'

Sheila leaned forward from the chair where a machine in a leather pouch was recording her heart – she too was not in the best health – and added: 'I remember we were stopped and asked to take part in a survey. We were asked to tick boxes for our earnings and I remember the top square said "£850 and above" and I ticked that. So we were in the top block.' Altogether better than the free frame and a handful of pound notes that the independents were getting.

There were four in the original team: Buttle, Bedwell, Dennis Talbot and Clive Parker. Talbot, who lives in a house owned by the Duke of Bedford at Woburn Park, said: 'We had amazing pride and ambition. When Mac [McLachlan] asked me what made me think I was better than the rest, I said – and this sounds awful now – I said I was going to be world champion. And I genuinely believed it.'

Guided by Frank Southall, who managed the remnants of the record-breaking team – now reduced to Ken Joy and Eileen Sherman – McLachlan prescribed a year of racing in Britain with trips to the world championships and anything else that came up, a year of British and international racing and then, in 1955, a year abroad to prepare for the Tour.

Buttle recalled: 'We always believed in ourselves but to find suddenly that you were riding against Coppi and Rik van Steenbergen and Bartali, and I rode against all them, well, bloody hell, you suddenly realised what you'd done. And it was odd when people asked for your autograph. But we were bike-riders; we lived in our own little world.'

In 1955 the team expanded from the six to which it had grown over two years to double that size, the potential Tour squad. The existing riders weren't consulted about who was brought in, Talbot says, and the decisions caused splits that never healed.

They were made by the new manager, Syd Cozens, winner of the 1934 London six-day and since brought in over Frank Southall's head from the failed BSA team 'because someone had a down on Frank at Hercules'. It is hard to find anyone with a good word for

Cozens. Buttle remembered: 'We'd gone down to a training camp on the Riviera and we were staying at a place called Les Issambres, near Marseille. This was 1955, the year we were to ride the Tour. In England we were the cream but abroad we were amateurs when it came to things like Milan–San Remo.'

Bedwell finished second to Jacques Anquetil at Fréjus and outsprinted André Darrigade in the Tour of Picardy. He was understandably pleased but, while Buttle describes him as 'the world champion we never had', it would be understandable if neither Anquetil nor Darrigade noticed.

My job was always to get Bedwell to the line because he was our sprinter and I'd work like hell to do that. And I remember I was tired and I said to Cozens that I was quite prepared to ride the next race but if there was a chance of having a rest instead, that would be good for me and the team. Next day McLachlan paid us a visit and Cozens said, 'This is Derek Buttle and he's pulled out of the next race' and that was the end of my hopes of riding the Tour.

Things were even odder for Talbot. He fell off and hurt, of all things, his little finger. 'It sounds so minor but it meant I couldn't hold the bars, so I didn't ride either,' he said.

The team were numbers 31 to 40 – Bedwell, Tony Hoar, Stan Jones, Fred Krebs, Bob Maitland, Ken Mitchell, Bernard Pusey, Brian Robinson, Ian Steel and Bev Wood. Robinson, by the way, described Cozens as 'a bandit'. They rode not as Hercules – Steel and Wood were brought in from Viking, Jones from BSA and Mitchell from Wearwell – but for Britain, in white jerseys with two black bands and a Union Jack on the shoulders. George Pearson, the editor of *Cycling*, predicted they'd achieve a place in the top twelve.

Pusey went on stage two, Wood on stage three along with Bedwell, who lost impossible ground after puncturing. Jones quit on stage seven, Steel on stage eight, Maitland on stage nine, and Krebs and Mitchell in the mountains on stage 11, Mitchell with saddle boils. Krebs came back to Britain and disappeared from cycling. Just two got to Paris, Robinson 29th at 1:57:10 and Hoar as lanterne rouge or last man at 6:6:01. Their mud-speckled bikes were displayed at the national cycle show at Earl's Court, the ashes of a great team.

Almost all the team was fired within weeks.

Talbot's understanding was that 'Hercules were faced with enormous costs and not enough receipts to make the books right'.

And they'd already been in problems with the tax people before, I think, and they weren't going to do it again by running the team another year.

They kept on four of us but then Mac came and told us we weren't staying either and he was such a gentleman that he cried as he told us. The other lads had been going round the show and fixing themselves up with sponsors. But by our time there was nobody left. All the teams were full.

Robinson left for the Continent and in 1958 became the first Briton to win a stage of the Tour. Talbot decided there was 'no way I was going abroad because of the drugs I'd seen there' and called it a day. Buttle considered pressing on but, just married, the only option was to race abroad 'and I'd have spent all I earned just to survive'. He just stopped cycling. Both marvel at what they did. Neither feels bitter.

The UCI had told the BLRC in 1953 it needed to create professional racing if it was to stand any chance of representing Britain instead of the NCU. Dave Orford says:

The BLRC brought in full pro racing in 1954 even though independent/amateur racing since 1947 had been highly successful, mainly as independents were only part-time pros who could ride events near home.

The League brought in full pro racing by 1954 but it did it with no infrastructure, meaning that they thought clubs would promote the events. Where was the money needed to come from? There were few events, and only one race was promoted on the occasional Sunday. The poorly supported independents were expected to travel all over the country at their own expense in order to be the supporting act to the Hercules team, which built up to twelve riders, with only 40 to 50 riders in the races.

Orford shows a bit of cheek here because, of course, he saw nothing wrong with amateurs being asked to be the chopping block of the independents in their own races, but nevertheless he has a good point.

'Frankly we just used to dominate everything when we raced in Britain,' Buttle says. 'Even when we split into A and B teams to make ourselves equal to the smaller teams, we just dominated everything. And in the end the other sponsors thought "What the hell?" It just wasn't worth it for them and they pulled out.'

'It was a fiasco,' says Orford.

By mid-1954 many of the independents were gone, also some of the track pros who had turned to the road after the demise of the John Dennis pro track-racing programme at Herne Hill. In the spring of 1956 I was out on the bike training, thinking my career was over, when I got an idea. I went home, got down to the local printer, and had 500 letterheads done – British Professional and Independent Cycling Association – making myself public relations officer. I had told no one of my plans.

My first letter was to the BLRC chairman, Eddie Lawton, stating that 1954-55 had been a disaster and that 'we' (only me) had formed the BPICA and that these were our demands and that if the BLRC could not accept them then we would have to go it alone.

To Orford's astonishment, the BLRC agreed to bring back the old system, of independents racing with amateurs, and Orford used the rest of the letterheads to tell everyone that "we" were back in business. When Orford writes to the cycling press even to this day, the letter will often be tailed 'ex-Ovaltine', because the personal outcome of his letterhead-printing scam was that he led a six-man team for the company from 1957 to 1963. The BLRC gave him an award for services to cycling in 1957.

11

MONSIEUR ROBINSON; MR TOM

The two surviving riders of that 1955 Tour made a living in different ways. Tony Hoar, still promoting events in Canada, finished last, 6:5:37 down. He was a popular *lanterne rouge* because he'd take on the big riders each day only to find his stocky build, ideal for Classics but not mountains or repeated stages, undid him after 80 miles. He would then struggle through the remaining 40 miles to reach the finish before exceeding the time limit and being eliminated. In Monaco he was so far back that only telling officials he was delayed by the crowds going home kept him in the race.

Whether the crowds really delayed him on the way to the finish, only he really knows. But they certainly delayed him on the way back to the hotel. Brian Robinson recalls that he loved meeting people, many of whom recognised him as the Tour's last rider, and that he'd chat to so many on the way back to the hotel after a stage that he'd be last to the massage table and last to the meal.

This affability meant Hoar picked up contracts for criteriums, where the crowd liked to applaud the plucky last man, but being *lanterne rouge* isn't a career. For that, Robinson was far the better placed.

The people in Stocks Bank Road, Huddersfield, probably pay little attention to the round-faced, grey-haired man they see most days on his bike. He still weighs what he did when he was at his peak, although he acknowledges that the distribution has changed. Even so, he still joins his friends for weekly 80-mile rides through the hills.

Some of the youngsters who can ride him off their wheel know who he is, of course, but time and memories pass quickly. To put him in context, you have to go back to 1937, coincidentally the first year that derailleurs were allowed in the Tour. That was when the first Britons rode the Tour, under the name of the Empire. In years long passed it was possible simply to enter the Tour de France, as you would any other race. By 1937 the Tour was accepting teams that represented their country. It had probably never occurred to the organiser, Henri Desgrange, that there were enough cyclists in Britain to form a team. And indeed there weren't, not of the right quality. The slow growth of massed-start racing, though, had persuaded at least a few of the country's best time-triallists that it was there, in events of the sort that Continentals but not Britons rode, that the future and fun of cycle racing lay.

Among them was Charles Holland, whose imagination had been fired by finishing fourth in that World Championship in Leipzig. Having reached the top in time-trialling and there being no further to go in amateur road-racing, he turned professional for Raleigh. By then, though, 'the three big heads – Raleigh, Hercules and BSA – had come to an agreement not to encourage professional racing because of the high cost involved. They were not really into the sporting side of the game, so I thought I would get away from them and I might as well go to the continent.'

With an ambitious, but less talented, Londoner called Bill Burl, he decided to write to enter the Tour de France. The toughest climb he had ever tackled was on the Isle of Man.

'They seemed very pleased to get my entry, the Tour de France. They thought I wouldn't stand it, that only a real professional could do it. I sent off my entry and I got a very good reply and they offered me this and that so I agreed. The costs were all met by the French people, the organisers of the Tour de France,' he said years later.

Holland was a favourite of the magazine *Cycling*, even if its journalists couldn't understand why he preferred this foreign racing to the traditions and purity of time-trialling. Desgrange, doubtless astonished to receive the two men's letters, had sent them contracts to ride. Holland wrote to *Cycling* to say he had signed. And he had, but for some reason Holland never understood, he wasn't accepted. A meeting in Birmingham with *Cycling*'s editor confirmed it because there in front of him was Desgrange's newspaper, *L'Auto*, and an English daily saying that Holland wouldn't after all be riding.

Given that Holland had turned professional and therefore could get back neither to time-trialling nor the newly born road-racing, he was in a fix. He sent a telegram, asking for clarification. Next day, through the Birmingham office again, he got a reply: 'Following your wire dated yesterday agree engagement if you agree yours – L'Auto.' The condition was that he and Burl ride not as individuals, as first planned, but in a team to represent the British Empire. With them would be a Frenchman called Pierre Gachon, who had emigrated to Canada and subsequently become a Canadian.

Burl went to Belgium to race and train, not appreciating that the Tour was only weeks away. He crashed in Ostend and broke a collarbone, which stopped him training. 'I don't think, to be honest, that he was a Tour rider,' was Holland's assessment. Neither man met Gachon until the day before the race started, although Holland quickly summed him up when he said: 'I think I'd have to think twice about [his] riding a second-class British event.'

Gachon didn't cope even with the first day and Burl was so far behind on the second that the organisers threw him out. Holland rode on for 2,000 miles until a broken pump stranded him on the day to Luchon. He punctured 30 metres behind the leaders on the col de Port and started work on a new tyre only to find the heat had warped the washer of his pump and made it useless.

He got it to half-pressure but punctured twice more and ran out of spare tyres. There was no Empire car, no Empire manager, and he had been adopted by the French, who called him Sir Holland. He ate with them, and they loaned him their mechanic and masseur. But the French car wasn't to hand at the crucial moment and nobody else would help. He stood by the roadside in despair.

A crowd of peasants had gathered around me, but they couldn't help me. A priest brought me a bottle of beer, and although it quenched my thirst it got me no further. After I had given up hope, a tourist came along and gave me a tubular touring tyre. I put it on, and in the excitement of the moment the rod of the pump broke. We blew the tyre hard with another pump but the tyre fitted so loosely on the rim that it came off with the fingers and so was unsafe. Another tyre was found that fitted a little better, and again I set off, but I had by then given up hope.

A carload of Belgian journalists, including Karel van Wijnendaele, the founder of the Tour of Flanders, tried to persuade him to continue. He wanted a lift but they refused, knowing it would mean his disqualification and therefore retirement. They offered him spare tyres instead and they even pushed him along from their seats in the car. In the end he accepted a lift from someone else, and he became just another footnote in the history of the Tour. It had proved an unhappy year, even if there was one smile left – Holland had quickly found a place in the hearts of not just French riders but French spectators. They were disappointed that he gave up and journalists following the race decided to give them the best tale they could. The next morning's papers reported that countrymen had pushed him in relays from one village to the next in the hope that he would get started again. Holland recalled:

> My riding in the Tour de France was a big disappointment to me because I felt I'd never been extended. I had a lot left in reserve. I didn't expect to win because we didn't have a team and I didn't have a manager. It seemed that they wanted me out of the race. They didn't give me a fair deal. You need a manager for a race like that, someone who can hand up your rations and your drinks, which you get through a lot of. But to have an organisation for one man wasn't in their thinking. They thought that nobody could ride without a manager. So they got all the publicity they could out of me but they wanted me out because what would people think if an individual rider with no support finished their race?

The assessment of George Pearson, a former editor of *Cycling*, was: 'As an amateur, he had been world-class but now, as a professional, he was having his first big race in the cash ranks in the world's toughest race. He had turned professional in May for the Wembley six-day, in which he had broken a collarbone and had to retire after two days. A further collarbone fracture in June (he tripped and broke the original bone before it had healed) caused him to miss a chance of mixing it with the continental stars in a circuit race at Crystal Palace, with the result that when he was invited to race in the Tour, he had been without any hard road-racing since the previous autumn.'

Holland came home and started training for the world championship, only to break his collarbone yet again. He didn't race again until 1938, when he broke the Land's End–London and Liverpool–Edinburgh records and, in 1939, Edinburgh–York. His career ended with the war, when he joined the Royal Corps of Signals. He ran two newsagents and a grocery shop in Birmingham, where he lived in Great Barr, took up golf, then returned to cycling to win the yearlong time-trialling championship for veterans in 1974 and 1975. He died in December 1989 and he's buried in the family grave at Aldridge in Staffordshire.

Charles Holland – the first Briton to ride in the Tour de France

That was the only encouragement that Robinson had in front of him when Hercules folded: that he and Hoar had finished the Tour where Holland, Burl and Gachon hadn't succeeded. They had already improved on history. 'It was a great feeling to finish the Tour,' Robinson said. 'You are out of the amateur status then. You have grown up.'

Grown up but still stuck in the nursery.

If I wanted to continue my career as a professional, I should have to organise my own programme. My friend Bernard Pusey and I and my wife, Shirley, motored down to Les Issambres [where Hercules had trained]. We arrived in the middle of a snowstorm. It kept on snowing for a month. Many of the early-season races in which we had hoped to pick up a few thousand francs to help with the expenses were cancelled.

When our rides were trouble-free, we rode well – but did not earn enough money. At first we were riding unsponsored. Then Georges Coupry took us into his newly formed La Perle team; no wages – just the bike and the chance of a bonus in the case of a win.

His agent, Daniel Dousset, appeared brilliant at arranging near-worthless contracts. His next move, to Hugo Koblet's Cilo team, brought him no wages except a little daily pocket money – but he at least kept him in work. The gain from such ubiquity was that reporters from *L'Équipe* recommended him to Jacques Goddet and Félix Lévitan, the organisers, as a good reserve for the Tour. That was how Robinson came to ride the Tour for Luxembourg in 1956.*

---

*A measure of how different things were in those days came in an announcement that Robinson placed in *Cycling* on January 17 1957. It said: 'Brian Robinson, who began his brilliant 1956 stage-racing saga with eighth place in the Tour of Spain, has been asked by the organisers to arrange four British professionals to join him in forming a mixed Portuguese-British team in this year's race. Riders interested in competing, or would-be professionals, should contact Brian Robinson as soon as possible at...'

He finished 14th in the Tour de France, his best place in five rides and the only Tour in which he had a free hand. In the others he was a domestique to someone greater and that, many assumed, would have been his role to the cantankerous climber Charly Gaul in the Luxembourg team. But it never happened.

Every hour I expected to be summoned to what I thought would be a certainty on the eve of the start – a conference to discuss tactics, allocation of prize money etc. But that meeting never took place. Had my orders been to nurse Gaul from Reims to Paris, with a promise of a cut of the total prize money won by the team at the end, then I would have obeyed those orders until I dropped.

I would willingly have obeyed them because I was certain Gaul could win the Grand Prix de la Montagne and so ensure £2,000 in the kitty. I therefore started the Tour a free man, free to get into newspaper headlines and so persuade the after-Tour organisers to engage me for their road and track meetings. Last year, the fact that I was one of the only two Englishmen ever to have finished the Tour had been sufficient to gain me contracts, but this time they would expect some outstanding performance before signing me on.

He came third on the first day, winning £60 for that, £100 for being the day's most aggressive rider, £20 in primes and a third of the £200 that Luxembourg won as the day's best team. It also made him, a Briton, the leader on general classification of the Luxembourg team with its star rider, Gaul, more than seven minutes down. Riders were still coming in after he, André Darrigade (with whom Robinson still goes skiing each winter) and Fritz Schaer had finished their lap of honour round the finishing circuit. He had made his mark.

That was 1956. The 1957 season had barely started when Robinson had his first professional win, in the Grand Prix de Nice. The race was one of a type that the Hercules team had ridden from Les Issambres, the sort of race now vanished. Until foreign travel became more common, and certainly before professional teams could race during the winter in Australia and the Middle East, riders and often whole teams would settle by the French Mediterranean coast. Towns such as Nice and Fréjus put on races for whoever wanted to ride, from the great stars to hopefuls like Robinson. You turned up and rode and when you'd had enough you got off and started again, slightly fitter, slightly slimmer, somewhere else next day.

For the stars they weren't important other than for training. But they were very important to the jobbing professionals whose contracts didn't start until Paris–Nice. If they could get a place in Paris–Nice, they could earn something early in the year.

Robinson entered at the last moment and lined up with the other 250. The race, like all season-openers, went along the coast and then into the hills before coming back down again. The hills behind the Mediterranean are not to be mocked, especially in spring and in an era when riders believed the best thing to do from October to January was nothing.

Robinson knew the main climb, the Turbie, and got to the front for the first climb. The 250 starters were down to a lead group of 50 after 15 kilometres of climbing. 'I was romping up the hill,' he recalled. 'I must have found one of those days when you just can't feel the pedals. Over the top we turned down a tricky little descent and at the bottom six of us found ourselves well clear of the bunch, and our reaction was immediate and we started working well together. I surveyed our chances and thought we were well off as Raymond Meyzencq, my team-mate, was one of the ace climbers in the Tour and I expected him to take his leave up one of the hills.'

Meyzencq's last chance was the eight-kilometre climb of the Mont de Mule. Robinson was scared of it, having never ridden it without being shot off, the last time only two days earlier in Genoa–Nice.

I thought if I can escape at the bottom of the hill, I can possibly stay away with Meyzencq when he comes by. So I dropped back a few yards and took a flyer. Much to my surprise, the only thing I had done was get rid of my own team-mate. I again hung back a few yards and snicked in a higher gear. I was off before they could do anything about it. I had a mile to go at the top and when I got there I had 25 seconds. I had 20 kilometres to go. Could I do it? In the early season one is never sure of just how good one's form is, but neither are the other riders, so it balances out. It was mostly downhill, so what could I lose if I got caught? I thought of all the things that could happen, like punctures, dogs in the road, going the wrong way and so on, but in the end I was in sight of the banner and I was very happy to cross that line and chalk up my first Number One.

Although no one can be absolutely certain, it was probably the first time a Briton had won a race on the Continent since James Moore won Paris–Rouen in the days of wooden wheels and iron tyres. Not forgetting the way he and the others had been abandoned by Hercules and how the sponsors had united to drop out of bike racing in Britain, he said his win was 'a reminder to some members of the British cycle industry who think that British cyclists haven't got what it takes'.

Robinson was now on a roll. He came third in Milan–San Remo behind Miguel Poblet of Spain and the little Belgian Fred De Bruyne, a man whose talent but relative lack of successes brought him the description of 'the champion who didn't leave his address'.

The chicanery behind Poblet's win still hurts. 'My manager, Raymond Louviot, had a tie-up in the cycle trade with Poblet. He told me that if Poblet was anywhere near me, it was my job to get him over the line first. I buggered off up a hill and then my manager came up and told me "Remember what I told you!" Poblet won. I was third. That is my biggest regret. If I had won, I would have been made for life.'

The background emerged later, that Poblet was riding the same make of bike as Robinson's St-Raphaël team, he said, and Louviot had been trying to get Poblet to join.

His stage win in the Tour in 1958 would have made him for life, too, had he been French or Belgian. Not a featherbedded life, perhaps, for the aspirations and rewards of the era were low, but other countries' riders would have been celebrities enough to open a bar, say, and be sure of custom late into life. But in Britain it meant little to other than fellow cyclists.

In fact, Robinson finished the stage, 170 kilometres from St-Brieuc to Brest, in second place. The story is that he attacked after 50 kilometres and took Jean Dotto and Arrigo Padovan with him. Robinson and Padovan entered the uphill finish together. Robinson came by him on the right but Padovan twice pushed him into the crowd and crossed the line first. Some press reports say Robinson shook Padovan's hand and then protested. Robinson denies it. 'I did not shake hands, and I only protested on the insistence of several journalist friends. Our team manager, Max Bulla [the first Austrian to wear the yellow jersey, which he did as a *touriste-routier* or private entrant in 1931], had already prepared the way for me with the commissaires.'

The judges demoted Padovan and gave the victory to Robinson. He said he was elated not only because of that, and because he'd won the 100,000 [old] francs prize as the day's most aggressive rider, but 'because it meant I would be sure of a good contract for the following year'. Any bitterness must have died because Robinson and Padovan meet each year at reunions of old riders in Burgundy.

'We always have a laugh about how he tried to push me into a ditch,' he says.

He profited from another quiet day next year and won by 20:06 at Chalon-sur-Saône after leading for 145 kilometres. His margin was so great that it eliminated the 1947 winner, Jean Robic. Normally a former winner would be allowed to stay in the race but Robic was getting his comeuppance for years of foul language and difficult behaviour. Robinson himself had faced elimination on the 14th stage, when he struggled in well after time with the help of the Irishman Shay Elliott. Many thought Elliott should have been allowed to stay in the race for his selflessness in helping Robinson, but the judges were heartless. The pain was all the worse for Elliott because Robinson was kept in the race under a rule that no rider in the first ten on general classification could be eliminated.

Robinson's last big success was the Dauphiné Libéré in 1961, which he won by more than six minutes. At 32 he returned to the family building business in Mirfield, West Yorkshire.

His career and that of his successor, Tom Simpson, crossed in 1960. Both were riding for Géminiani's St-Raphaël team (sometimes but falsely described as the first team with a sponsor from outside the bike industry; the first in fact was International Totalisator Pools, which backed the ITP team in Britain from 1947). It was Robinson's last Tour and he finished 26th; Simpson came 29th.

Brian Robinson and Tom Simpson:
Tour de France, 1960

Simpson achieved more than Robinson ever did, including the 1965 World Championship and in 1962 the yellow jersey of the Tour de France, if only for a day. But his memory is more muddied, given that he died with drugs coursing round his body on Mont Ventoux and that evidence exists of races bought and sold. There are still many who prefer to think that Simpson was innocent, that if he took drugs – which he admitted and which his autopsy made undeniable – it was only because everyone else did. And there are those who consider Simpson as not only as big a cheat as everyone else but the one prepared to cheat heavily enough for it to cost him his life.

The irony is that there are many riders who took as much, who risked as much, who now deny that they ever did and are regarded as heroes. Had Simpson lived, the drugs would never have been heard of and he would have become as cuddly a senior statesman of cycling as Reg Harris was. In that way, Barry Hoban, his team-mate in that fatal 1967 Tour, is right when he says: 'The only mistake the man made was to die.'

Simpson was a weedy, beak-nosed rider of astonishing ambition. As a 16-year-old he wrote to Charles Pélissier for advice and a place on a training camp in Monte Carlo; he asked George Berger, a French-speaker in the Redhill club in Surrey, to translate Louison Bobet's *En Selle*; and when he saw national service approaching, he skipped the country in 1959 and went to France in an era when cars were still loaded aboard ferries by crane and 'abroad' truly was another place.

He applied for a semi-professional licence almost immediately and had a professional licence within a year. Letters home to George Shaw, his friend in Sheffield and whose name will reappear shortly, show he spent his time winning races – 28 in his first year as a professional – shagging girls and worrying about life as a foreigner in France.

The country himself didn't trouble him as much as a rule which insisted most of any professional team come from the country in which it was registered. A French team had to have mostly French riders, a Belgian team would be almost all Belgian, and so on. There had been no British teams since Hercules, so Simpson had to prove himself good enough not only to get into a team but to displace one of the home riders, as well. He was up against both home-born talent with home-based support and comforts, and natural chauvinism. And once he was in one of those teams, he had to fight to hold his place. That was a theme of his career and in the end it killed him.

Simpson's problem was that his ambition was bigger than his body. Vin Denson, who went to France about the same time and became his closest friend, told me: 'We often used to have a laugh with Tom about his hollow chest. It was considered to be hereditary, because with his family's mining history, and the lack of oxygen down in the pits, all their lungs were underdeveloped. He had a really good pair of athletic legs, but his chest was always a worry to us. We never ever thought that he did actually get sufficient oxygen in the tiny lungs that he must have had.'

The physiology may be shaky but it does describe Simpson's physique. He finished his first Tour a wreck, having crashed in Brussels on the first day, and he so overdid the post-Tour criteriums that took riders repeatedly from northern Belgium to southern France and back in a dash for cash that he ended up in hospital in Paris.

His lightness meant he could ride 28-spoke wheels, the preserve of trackmen, but it made him a poor sprinter. The only way he felt sure of winning was to attack alone. The lone charges were always spectacular, occasionally successful, more often disastrous, almost always self-destructive. He dominated Liège–Bastogne–Liège in 1963 only to be caught and dropped by the bunch a mile from the finish. He spent 40 miles alone in the 1964 Milan–San Remo before being caught just before the finish on the Poggio climb; he led Paris–Roubaix for 56 minutes and lost it two miles from the end.

Of Milan–San Remo, Roger St Pierre wrote: 'When I finally spotted him plodding slowly down the last half-mile to the line, he looked terrible. His face was drawn, fatigue oozing out of every line. His eyes looked lifeless. He was completely, utterly spent. I helped him to the changing rooms and even had to untie his shoelaces for him. He was quivering with fatigue, his eyes red-rimmed and unable to focus.'

Will Fotheringham, when he was preparing to write about Simpson's life in *Put Me Back on my Bike*, agonised about how he was to frame those and other spectacular, debilitating and undeniably courageous rides against the belief that they were the behaviour of a rider so high on drugs that he barely knew what he was doing. The whole point of taking amphetamines was that they gave a wild, obsessive, all-absorbing bravery, strong to and beyond the point of recklessness.

Jacques Goddet, said of him: 'A champion, he wanted victory too badly. We often asked ourselves if this athlete, who at work often appeared in pain, had not committed some errors in the way he looked after himself.' For an obituary, especially a French one of the 1960s, it was damning. The codes are all there: 'we *often* asked ourselves…', '*often* appeared in pain…', '*errors* in the way he looked after himself.' For an obituary written by the Tour de France organiser while Simpson's body was still in the morgue, it was extraordinary.

It's hardly fair to say that Simpson would never have died if Hercules had stayed in sponsorship, or at least if another sponsor had taken its place. But it plays a part. Simpson never declined the mantle of 'riding for Britain' that British journalists put on him, nor objected to being quoted with remarks such as 'I must ride well because people in England [sic] expect it of me'. In a way, it made his death and the evidence of his drug-taking harder to bear, because he had accepted the role of representing all the cyclists in Britain who invested their faith in him.

When Simpson said all that, it was often angled at attracting a British sponsor. If he could be 'riding for Britain' both nationally and commercially, he would no longer have to fight for his place in the team and the riders appointed to ride for him, while often weaker than he'd have had abroad, would have been loyal. They, after all, would also have had nowhere else to go.

Simpson started his professional years with the fledgling St-Raphaël team but spent his best with Peugeot, a company that had been in team sponsorship since the start of the century. He won the World Championship in 1965 while sponsored by Peugeot and illegally wore his Peugeot rather than his Great Britain jersey to the podium when he accepted his rainbow jersey. He then wore that jersey with Peugeot's name embroidered on it. For decades riders had honoured the rainbow by keeping it unsullied by advertising.

All that was aimed at keeping him as Peugeot's star man. He was trying harder than a Frenchman would have to. The trouble was that a man who could have expected fat appearance contracts as World Champion got very little because he broke his leg in a skiing accident. He rode the Herne Hill Good Friday meeting in 1966 soon after recovering, one leg noticeably thinner than the other, and tried to demand that the home professionals riding against him let him win.

A cocky south Londoner called Dave Bonner made a point of both disagreeing and of beating him, which the crowd thought wonderfully exciting, although it knew nothing of the significance. 'He told me I should let him win, that he was the one the people had come to see,' Bonner said. 'I told him he'd been a struggling professional once and I told him to beat me if he could. He wasn't happy.' Nor were the home professionals who, not for the last time, resented the money they believed Simpson or other stars were being paid to use them as chopping blocks.

Fixing races was no novelty for Simpson. It was certainly true that he was the big draw at Herne Hill but I know, because I was one of them, that spectators were thrilled to see 'plucky' Bonner nipping by him, tweaking the lion's tale. It made for a better afternoon. It made for a harder time for Simpson, it emerged later, because he was earning so little then that he was struggling to pay his bills.

Look at pictures of Simpson's win in the Tour of Flanders in 1961 and you can see that Nino Defillipis, the second man, has his hands on the brakes before the line. It could be confusion because the finish banner had blown down, and certainly there were protests afterwards, but undeniably his fingers were on the brakes.

Look at Ghent–Wevelgem the following year. Benoni Beheyt is sprinting up the right of the road and holding another Belgian, Michael van Aerde, against the barrier. Simpson is in the middle of the road in his long-sleeved Peugeot shirt. His mouth is theatrically openmouthed, his elbows out... and he has his fingers on both brakes five meters before the line.

In 1965 Simpson won London–Holyhead, a monster of a race that counted for nothing on the Continent and even had to stop for traffic lights on the A5 but which was important if Simpson was to find a British sponsor. The lead group reached Holyhead after more than ten hours' racing and Simpson won, as everyone expected. But pictures once more tell a story. Just behind him, the Irishman Shay Elliott has his fingers on the brakes.

Cycling dismissed it as automatic reaction to losing the sprint. Vin Denson, however, says that he and others had fixed the race for

Simpson but that the leading home-based rider, Albert Hitchen, wasn't in on the deal. Hitchen's talent had been underestimated and Elliott was forced to brake to stop him coming by and winning. Such things happened in the roughhouse of professional cycling and Simpson doubtless wasn't alone. But he was in an unusual position because Peugeot had been disappointed with his publicity-free year in 1966. Eddy Merckx was threatening his position as team leader and Simpson would have gladly left to take up offers elsewhere, particularly from Felice Gimondi's Salvarani team, but Peugeot wouldn't release him.

Then came an unusual combination of events. In July 1966, France passed *la loi Herzog*, which made drug-taking not just an offence in a sport which preferred to do nothing, but a breach of the law in a state which intended to act. In particular, it acted in Bordeaux just before the Pyrenees in that year's Tour. It descended on the race and conducted drug tests against those who would oblige. Many just refused, claiming tests were a breach of their personal liberty and that their organisation was haphazard and shoddy, which was true. Next morning they rode as far as the university area of La House. These days it's where the modern *autoroute* distributes traffic for Paris, Barcelona and the Mediterranean. And there they got off and walked.

Taking part along with everyone else was Simpson. He was, according to the new Tour doctor Pierre Dumas, a regular drug-taker, a claim the doctor made several times in interviews with *L'Équipe* and elsewhere. Other riders since have confirmed it, and said that Simpson talked about it openly among fellow professionals, but that in taking stimulants he was far from unusual. Nevertheless, Simpson was cautious about the strike, saying: 'It gives publicity to the anti-doping affair that we don't need.'

The all-stop, and the way the riders let a tinpot Italian called Tommaso De Pra take the yellow jersey next day, upset the organisers more than anyone could have imagined. Félix Lévitan swore that team sponsors had whipped it all up and said they were as big a pain to him in 1966 as they had been to Henri Desgrange in 1930. Therefore he would do what Desgrange had done and do away with sponsored teams and insist riders represent their country.

In practice, the punishment lasted only two years, but just one year was enough for Simpson. It played to his advantage because he was no longer subservient to Peugeot and he would have the British team he always wanted. It was supported by the banana company, Fyffes, which never mentioned the race again, given what happened, but which at the time was considered a possible permanent sponsor.

Felice Gimondi told Simpson that he would take him into the Salvarani team when the Peugeot contract expired that autumn provided he did a good ride in the Tour. Simpson's agent, Daniel Dousset – who, together with his smaller rival Roger Piel, had all French racing carved up – told him that whatever happened with Salvarani, Simpson's reputation was so low that he could expect few criterium contracts unless he got a podium place in Paris or, failing that, won a stage.

The importance of criteriums in that period can't be understated. It was where riders earned most of their money, sometimes more than they would from their retainers and prizes together. Dousset and Piel controlled the whole system, took ten per cent of everything, and could include or shut out riders at will. No matter how mighty a rider, Dousset, in particular, was mightier still.

That was the atmosphere in which Simpson went to the Tour. At home, nobody knew anything of it. The issue in Britain was simple: there was a British team in the Tour, hip-hip-hooray. The undercurrents were as deadly and as invisible as they always are.

The stage that Simpson chose for his big day was Mont Ventoux. The mountain rises above Provence like a whale, domed, wooded to three-quarter distance and then bleak. Its difficulty lies neither in its steepness or length – there are many worse – but in the odd climate. The wooded area can be stifling on hot days, when there never seems to be enough air, and the exposed final kilometres come as a sudden and baking shock after the hairpin at the Chalet Reynard. Riders feared and hated it.

Jean Mallejac collapsed on Mont Ventoux in 1955 with his drug-ridden brain still turning his pedals. He 'struggled, gesticulated, shouted for his bike, and wanted to escape [from the ambulance] so much that he had to be strapped down'. The novelist and

111

sportswriter Antoine Blondin said of it: 'We have seen riders reduced to madness under the effect of the heat or stimulants, some coming back down the hairpins they thought they were climbing, others brandishing their pumps and accusing us of murder.'

In other words, by the time Simpson rode it in 1967, history, tradition, fear and ambition demanded a hefty quantity of drugs.

That morning the Tour doctor, Pierre Dumas, went for a walk with the French journalist Pierre Chany. It was 7 a.m. and already hot. Outside the Hôtel Noailles, Chany said, Dumas sniffed the air and said: 'The heat's going to be awful today: if the lads stick their noses in the *topette* [take drugs], we could have a death on our hands.'

At the foot of Mont Ventoux is the village of Bédoin. Simpson stole a bottle of cognac. That wasn't unusual: at that time it was a shabby Tour tradition to jump off your bike, run into a café, steal whatever you fancied and run out again. Bar owners sent the bill to the Tour organisers. What was unusual is that star riders usually got team-mates to do the plundering for them. It was a measure of Simpson's concern that on 13 July 1967, he did it himself.

Why cognac? Riders would take anything to make themselves ride better and alcohol was both a stimulant and a painkiller. But more particularly, it made amphetamine more effective.

The first kilometres from Bédoin barely rise and Simpson had no trouble regaining the bunch as it rode cautiously towards the real climb. It had already ridden around 100 miles in a *canicule* – a heatwave – and many riders had drugged themselves just for that.

Two riders shared Simpson's plan for Mont Ventoux. The first was Raymond Poulidor, a good climber who had never yet won the Tour and saw this as his chance. The other was a still better climber called Julio Jiménez, who could win the mountains competition. Nearing the Chalet Reynard, they were joined by Felice Gimondi and together they reached the T-junction outside the bar and turned left to the summit.

Then came Simpson. A hundred metres behind him was the Frenchman Lucien Aimar, who had punctured, and Herman van Springel and Desiré Letort. They passed Simpson soon after the Chalet. Aimar remembered: 'The heat was suffocating. I offered him a drink but he didn't hear me. He had a totally empty look, and the extraordinary thing was that he started shooting his mouth off at me. He took 250 metres out of me. I said to him: "Tom, don't be an arsehole!" But he didn't respond. A moment later, he was on my back wheel. I heard a cry, but I didn't see him fall.'

Harry Hall, the mechanic, was behind Simpson in the team's white Peugeot. The doors had been replaced by canvas panels to keep it cooler. He said:

His riding became jerky. He lost his flow. He rode criss-crossing across the climb, the way that amateurs do. And then he rode to the left-hand side of the road, and there's quite a sheer drop. If you go over, you don't stop on one of those things. He did this a couple of times and I was ready to jump out of the car when he swung back and hit the bank on the right-hand side.

His speed had dropped off and he fell over against the bank, on his right-hand shoulder. I remember well, I said, 'That's it, Tom. That's it for you!' and I undid his toe straps. And at this point he burst into 'No, no'. He wouldn't have that. 'Get me up, get me up.' So he was quite coherent. He said, 'I want to go on. Get me up, get me straight.'

Hall lifted him, with the manager, a London car-hire salesman called Alec Taylor whose name but not his accent disguised Anglo–Belgian origins. They re-tightened his straps, told him to concentrate, and pushed him back on the road. He rode another 300 metres and collapsed again.

Down the mountain, Pierre Dumas was watching the main race through the open sun roof of his own Peugeot. A gendarme on his blue motorbike told him there'd been a *pépin* – a spot of bother – and cleared the way for him to reach Simpson. Hall and the other mechanic, Ken Ryall, had prised Simpson's fingers off the handlebars, where they had locked, and had lain him on the roadside. Hall had started mouth-to-mouth resuscitation.

Dumas took over, giving Simpson oxygen and massaging his heart. Hall said Simpson 'looked absolutely dreadful' and Dumas said later that he was already dead. He wasn't saving a life, he was struggling to restart one. The medical helicopter landed on the uneven rocks of the mountainside, its rotors turning fast to give it stability. The official report said that it took off again at 4.40 p.m. and arrived at the Sainte-Marthe hospital at 5.15. Simpson was confirmed dead on arrival and the news was announced to the Tour press room at 5.40. It was shortly afterwards that Sid Saltmarsh, reporting the race for *Cycling* and the *Sun*, invented the last words which have been attributed to Simpson ever since: 'Put me back on my bike.'

His death led the television news. Drugs weren't mentioned, then or for some days. Then Jim Manning, a columnist for the *Daily Mail* who once referred to athletes peeing into bottles as 'a jolly thought', uncovered the truth. Simpson had been declared dead from overwork, sunstroke and dehydration, which was true but not the whole truth. He had drugged himself, Manning said, so he no longer knew what he was doing. There had been drugs in his blood and more in two small bottles in the pockets of his jersey.

More, Manning suggested, France had delayed penalising other drugged Tour riders because it was too embarrassed to do it in midsummer and ruin a major tourist draw.

Alan Gayfer, the editor of *Cycling*, began a public subscription for a stained-glass window in the church at Harworth, the Nottinghamshire mining village where Simpson had grown up. When that proved too expensive, he and his boss Peter Bryan hit on the idea for a marble monument on the roadside where he'd died. It's still there, a draw for thousands of cyclists a year who leave as a tribute any old bottles or caps they happen to be carrying.

Nobody knows who owns it. It doesn't belong to *Cycling* because the subscription was public and paid by anonymous donors. There was no formal appeal body or charity. The memorial doesn't belong to the Simpson family, although *Cycling* editor Robert Garbutt would like it to. And it doesn't belong to Bédoin – although the village's barkeepers tidy it up once in a while – nor to the *départment* in which it stands, although its council gave permission and possibly, although it's not clear, the land. The issue has become important because, approaching 40 years after the event, the monument's concrete base has started to crumble.

The whole business ended in a legal vacuum, with no owner for the monument, no inquest in Britain, not even an inquiry by the BCF into why one of its team had dropped dead in circumstances which hardly left the BCF in a good light. Len Unwin, the federation's secretary, happened to be on holiday. That left the racing secretary, Bryan Wotton, to handle the thousands of calls.

'The whole world fell on our little office,' he said. 'By the time it had all finished, I don't think it had occurred to anyone that there hadn't been an inquiry.'

By then, though, although he could never have guessed, Simpson had set in train events that would lead to the biggest team run from Britain that the nation has ever known. He would have been too old to ride in it but that Simpson had a hand is undeniable. But we'll come to that later.

12

MILK MAKES A MAN OF YOU

Simpson and the other pioneers of the 1950s and 1960s – Robinson, John Andrews, Vin Denson ('always laughing, one of the smiling giants of the world' according to Ron Kitching), Alan Ramsbottom, Vic Sutton, Derek Harrison, Barry Hoban and so on – would never have had to go abroad had Britain had a national tour of its own. It could have led to professional teams and a professional calendar. It could have put cycling on enough of a publicity footing for sponsorship that could have provided a living and not just a frame, jersey and a couple of quid from a bike shop. 'Could' rather than 'would', of course.

The BLRC wanted professional racing but it never successfully got beyond independents. The year it converted its independents to professionals, to help woo the UCI into recognising it as the national body, it killed off what it had, as Dave Orford said.

Prizes were barely worth the effort. Britain's first all-pro race, the 108-mile South Elmsall Spring Classic in 1954, rewarded Dennis Talbot with £5. Paris–London (the stage from Kent to London was a time-trial) paid George Fleming £15, 'while the winner of the 440-yard handicap at the supporting track meeting won a prize of equal value,' says Chas Messenger. Even the Victory Marathon and its successors were paid for largely by IOUs from the BLRC and the private money and time of the officials who ran it.

The first commercial sponsorship of the Tour of Britain was £500 given by the *News of the World* for the 1947 Brighton–Glasgow. In less than a year the paper pulled out again, concerned at the BLRC's infighting. The 1950 race was backed by *Sporting Record*, followed by the *Daily Express* in 1952 (the year the NCU voted 50-20 at its general council to join the BLRC in running road-races). But that too drowned in bickering.

John Dennis says: 'The most effective sponsor of the Tour of Britain, the *Daily Express*, was lost as a result of the constant bickering between rival officials and organisations. I was the press officer to the *Express* publicity director, Albert Asher, and saw it all happen. He was upset by the petty disagreements and decided to support the new Formula 1 motor-racing instead.'

Ken Russell's memory is: 'After the 1952 Tour I was invited to the Fleet Street offices of the *Daily Express* where Mr Asher told me they were delighted with the '52 Tour. It was the incident at the after-race dinner of the 1953 Tour which soured the relationship between the *Express* and BLRC, when officials of the NCU had been invited and were seated at the top table. Some of the BLRC officials walked out; in hindsight perhaps they should not have done, but how could anyone expect them to sit down with men who had vilified the BLRC for the past ten years?'

The *Express* pulled out after 1953 and sponsorship was taken up by Quaker Oats for 1954. And then in 1958, waved away from Alexandra Palace to Skegness by the comedian Norman Wisdom, came the Milk for Stamina Tour of Britain.

The Milk Marketing Board was a sales monopoly for English and Welsh dairy farmers. It was the ideal sponsor for something as wholesome and health-demanding as the Tour of Britain and the only surprise, in retrospect, is that it didn't occur to anyone earlier. In fact, the approach was to sponsor not a race but riders. Dave Orford's idea was that the MMB should advertise 'Drink more milk' on the sleeves of all the teams in Britain. Every weekend it could advertise that one of its riders had won, thanks to milk. In return it would pay £10 to the rider or riders who'd done it.

The MMB's publicity officer, Reg Pugh, asked Orford to the board's offices at Thames Ditton in Surrey. Orford says: 'At the end of the discussion he stated that the MMB would prefer to sponsor a major international marathon. So the Milk Race, the Tour of Britain, was born, starting in 1958 and lasting for 35 years, the longest cycle sponsorship in the UK ever.'

The arrangements were taken up by the BLRC, in its last months before merging with the NCU. Chas Messenger, elected race organiser, was joined by Eddie Lawton and Les Keith and gave Pugh figures that Messenger concedes were 'conjured out of thin air' by the treasurer, Ruben Smith.

It was really a Tour of England and Wales, for the MMB's monopoly didn't extend to Scotland. But a tour, in the French sense of *circuit*, it certainly was. Just as the first Tours de France ran round the edges of the country, so the first Milk Race followed the coasts of England and Wales, missing only East Anglia (too flat), south-west Wales (because central Wales was harder) and Kent and Sussex (because the race had to get back to London from Bournemouth).

Orford, still an independent for Ovaltine, made sure his race was for semi-professionals as well. He says: 'Things went very well for the domestic independents right up until the second Milk Race in 1959.' The irony is deliberate.

Benny Foster, the manager of the very strong Elswick-Hopper team, 'permitted' his two top riders, Ron Coe and Harry Reynolds, to be included in the England team, with the other Hopper riders distributed in other regional teams, plus John Geddes in the Army team.

Obviously, it was a great honour to be in the England team and Foster assumed that Coe would become leader of that team. Sadly for Foster, the amateur international Bill Bradley, also in the England team and a superb climber, took a big lead on everyone else in the race over a dreadfully hard stage four, Whitley Bay to Morecambe. He was now ten minutes in the lead.

Foster was not involved with the race because Tiny Thomas filled the role of England team manager. However, Foster concocted a plan for the England riders Coe and Reynolds to hamper Bradley in order that the fellow Hopper rider, Geddes, who was in second place on general classification, could escape in a breakaway in order to steal the lead from Bradley.

Thomas, who was no fool, spotted what was going on and at the end of that stage Coe and Reynolds were removed from the England team and sent home in disgrace. And Bradley, rightly, went on to win the race.

Officialdom were so alarmed at team-mates having conflicting professional and patriotic pulls that independents never again rode the Milk Race – 'thanks to a greedy, self-important man, Benny Foster,' says Orford – and the very people whom Orford planned to help with MMB sponsorship were the ones to be denied it.

Messenger ran the race from 1958 to 1964, exhibiting a love of distance and hills. There was no limit to how far riders could be made to go and in 1962 it took Norman Baty more than seven hours to win a stage from Seaburn to Morecambe. The route went across the Pennines and brought bitter criticism from riders that most had struggled to survive, let alone race.

The money was greater than earlier BLRC events had ever known, but riders were still accommodated in bed-and-breakfast venues and cheap hotels. The public address was a loud hailer on top of a van; following vehicles were private cars or borrowed furniture vans with banners stretched across the front. The race ran into traffic jams, one so bad that riders sat by the roadside until a monster hold-up cleared in Devon.

Bill Bradley leads the 1960 Tour of Britain through Worksop

In time, it became a slick organisation, said to rank in prestige only behind the Tour de l'Avenir, the amateur–independent race that shadowed the Tour de France, and the Peace Race that crossed Poland, Czechoslovakia and East Germany.

The east European countries had always been good to the BLRC, not bothering too much about whether it was affiliated to the UCI. Ian Steel won the Peace Race in 1952 and mutual respect was born, helped by the BLRC's links with the Fédération Sportive et Gymnastique du Travail. Communist enthusiasm for the Milk Race peaked in 1980 when Russian riders took the first four places, and had five in the top six.

The Russian impact went beyond the tough way they rode; the organisers were compelled to book an extra place for teams from the USSR, which were accompanied by an extra official whose role was never defined. He was regarded as the KGB man responsible for making sure nobody defected. And certainly the social distance that Russian riders maintained from the rest of the race emphasised the terror he imposed.

The Russians, though, never won by as great a margin as a self-deprecating Potteries joiner called Les West. This affable, slightly shy man rode a bike as though he'd just borrowed it from someone else. The more he complained that he felt unwell or he'd lost interest in winning, the more he was certain to ride off and win. If the day was wet, windy and dark, so much the better. In 1967 he won by 17:47.

West's humble attitude extended to the way he travelled, in an unimposing workman's van which, as a nervous driver, he rarely took much beyond 50 mph. He was so well known for it that the London rider Reg Barnett, a cross between Arthur Daley and his minder, made a point of driving him across London so fast that he hid in fright.

'He bloody did,' West said. 'He had a big Zephyr and his two wheels on the driving side were permanently over the white line, and he just kept driving down the middle and everything coming to him just had to keep shooting over, which was typical of Reg, as I found out. I was absolutely terrified. I'll never forget that journey.'

West always preferred to drive slowly home to his wife Pat – 'my lady' – than stay the night away. A man that cautious wasn't likely to give up working, and it was going to work that almost had him thrown out of the 1967 Milk Race – the one he won by a record margin – before it had started. He said:

All the time as an amateur I used to have a full-time job and go training three times a week at night. Which is hard to believe these days, but it's the gospel truth. I think we should have been there on the Friday and I didn't get picked up until Saturday dinner time. And, of course, we were a day late when we got to Brighton. We got lost going through London – me, Brian Rourke and the driver – so we just rolled up as innocent as anything and they said we couldn't ride.

Well, that was the night before, so I don't know what all the fuss was about. Maurice Cumberworth [the organiser] said it, like. We had a bit of an argument, but the thing was you couldn't really argue too much. Bob Thom [the manager] told us to shut up and get out of the way, and they had a meeting.

But they were going to say, right, half the team weren't going to ride. I mean, the Great Britain team were going to *not* ride. Can you imagine that on the Continent? I was one of the top riders in the race and they were going to stop me riding. I mean, on the Continent they'd come and fetch me, wouldn't they? And when I got there, they'd say 'Well, thank God you've turned up; you had us worried'. But that's the difference. I laugh about it now.

He laughs, too, at the way his innocent personality lined him up for tricks pulled by more knowing members of the team.

We used to have Kenny Hill, Pete Matthews and Billy Perkins, three Scousers. Instead of being tucked up in bed, we were out on the town, in restaurants and having a laugh. And I think that took a lot of the pressure of the race off us. I mean, I don't think they'd allow it now but we just used to be out on the town.

In them days you had a meal [at the race hotel] but it was never enough. So they used to give you extra money to go out and have a meal. And, of course, we were in the ruddy cafés and restaurants at all hours, and having all the waitresses in stitches.

We used to go down in a taxi and then, the buggers, they used to get out of the taxi and all run off and say they weren't paying. And I'd have to pay the money. We went in Madame Tussaud's waxworks at Morecambe by the back entrance and got kicked out of there. And we'd go in cafés and Pete Matthews never used to pay half the time. He used to sneak out and then the waitress used to say, 'If you can get out of here without paying, you're welcome to try.' And the buggers got out all the same. We used to walk around town instead of resting. It was like a fortnight's holiday, really, except we had to work again next morning, like. And it was quite funny.

West came second to Eef Dolman – a man caught some time later defrauding a dope control – in the 1966 World Championship in Germany. He insists that while the Dutch made a fuss of Dolman, a BCF official came up to him and said, 'Good ride, son. What's your name?'

The name was noticed by Jacques Anquetil, though, and he said he'd like West in his Bic team and told his British domestique, Vin Denson, to fix it. West says: 'Vin Denson came over to our house to see me, and I said, "Right, January the first." And he said, "I'll get your contract sent over," and it never came.' West, being West, never thought to ask what had happened. He still doesn't know why it didn't come, although he wonders whether reports that he was going to join the Dutch Willem II team may have reached Anquetil and ended his interest.

In fact, West wasn't going to join Willem II and he's still in two minds about whether he wanted to race as a professional abroad anyway. On the one hand there is professional ambition that makes a rider yearn for the best races. On the other was the reluctance to leave the Potteries and an equally strong reluctance to ride in a world riddled by drug-taking.

West had spent a year in Holland and he raced in criteriums in Belgium, where he saw riders with their eyes banging on their noses, riding faster than in any Classic. That was more than he could stand. He came home and joined a domestic team, Holdsworth, in 1969. It paid him £1,000 a year, about what he earned with British Telecom and a good retainer for a pro in Britain.

I saw him win his first event, a stage race on the Isle of Wight, and old habits hadn't died. 'That's my first win and probably my last,' he said. In 1970 he finished fourth in the World Professional Championship at Leicester, beaten by Jempi Monsere of Belgium (who died in a race crash soon afterwards), the Italian Tour winner Felice Gimondi and the Dane Leif Mortensen. Monsere outsprinted the others easily and West was going for third place when Gimondi shut him out. He'd done much of the work in the break, reasoning that sixth place – there were six clear – would be better than to finish in the middle of the bunch that was only 20 seconds behind.

West won the British professional championship twice, in 1970 and 1975 and called it a day in 1982. 'It was travelling, travelling, travelling, and the travelling got me down more than the riding. Plus the fact that when we were riding, there was only about ten of us racing and the other 20 sat in there watching and came past at the finish. And nine out of ten of the races weren't suitable to me anyway – up and down sea fronts, or something short. Like, as an amateur, you could pick your course, couldn't you?'

West's fascinating innocence in life extended to life after racing. Taking his daughter Joanna to a local running track, he had to wait two hours before he could bring her back. Next time he joined in, wearing plimsolls and ordinary trousers. Four weeks later he was keeping up. He then ran his first London marathon in 2:44, a time that most runners dream of.

He didn't run for long: 'I'm permanently injured; I'm always injured when I run – it's a silly sport.' But the effect among his fellow runners in their mid-40s was startling.

The life didn't go out of the Milk Race when West left but much British interest did. The Dutch sent stronger and stronger teams and won all but one year from 1969 to 1974. A home tour in which domestic riders no longer figure lacks gloss, as the French found with their own tour after Bernard Hinault. When it wasn't the Dutch, it was the Russians again. *Cycling* reported the Londoner Bob Downs saying: 'We were like amateurs against pros. The whole Russian team used to get on the front and not let anyone else in. The only way you could stand a chance was to ride as near as possible to them and wait for them to make a mistake.' After the Dutch had finished winning, the Russians took over every year but two from 1977 to 1984.

The only British relief was Bill Nickson's success in 1976, when he won by five seconds from his countryman Joe Waugh.

The last years of the Milk Race were a repeat of the way the Tour of Britain had started – a mixture of amateurs and paid riders. The paid riders were now called professionals rather than independents but the ideas of the BLRC and of Dave Orford had come full circle. Sadly, for some, they turned what had been a world-class amateur race into a second-rate pro-am one.

The Milk Marketing Board was disbanded after it fell foul of European monopoly rules and Chris Lillywhite's win in 1993 brought the Milk Race to an end.

The race's success was its own undoing; the name Milk Race had become so closely associated with the Tour of Britain that many potential sponsors weren't interested for years. A professional race, the Kellogg's Tour, grew up alongside it and even outlasted it. But sponsors as dedicated as the Milk Marketing Board have proved impossible to find and the story of national tours since then has been of promising starts foiled by the reluctance of backers to stay involved.

The chase for more backers, for another national tour, goes on. Time, though, is against it. So too is the traffic – much busier now than when the Tour of Britain started. And the attitudes of chief constables are near-impossible. The Milk Race had become an institution, almost a national treasure. It continued to an extent under its own momentum and because most police areas had had some experience of it in their area. New races don't have that benefit.

13

THE FIRING SQUAD

The grand gestures of the bike trade in the 1950s were its death throes. The pro team didn't finish Hercules but it did little to keep it going. The same went for BSA and the rest. By 1958 BSA, Triumph, New Hudson and Sunbeam were part of Raleigh; Hercules, Armstrong, James, Norman, Sun and the chain company Brampton and others had all been taken over by Raleigh's rival, the British Cycle Corporation.

BCC was in turn owned by Tube Investments, which ran the bike conglomerate to protect its market. Its chairman was John Reith, the terrifying, heavy-browed and scar-faced 1st Baron Reith of Stonehaven who became Director General of the fledgling BBC in 1927. He left there in 1938 to run Imperial Airways, the start of a steady decline in his career which took him to Tube Investments after the war. Although brilliant in his conception of public-service broadcasting against the commercialism of its American equivalent, he was dour and unmoving and hardly the man to put fire into a dying bike industry.

A sternly religious man with old-world attitudes, Reith insisted the BBC broadcast nothing on Sunday mornings and only solemn music in the afternoons. He was forced out of that when pirate stations opening on the French coast took his audience, but he stuck to his principles and was said to fire employees who divorced. Persuaded not to dispense with one broadcaster, he thundered: 'He can stay, but ensure that he never reads the epilogue.' The epilogue was the end-of-day religious reading on which Reith insisted.

Reith could afford to wait. He watched Raleigh open a third factory in Nottingham – the guest was the equally abrasive Bernard Montgomery, the wartime military leader and Eisenhower's troublesome deputy for D-Day – and slowly overextend itself.

'The future was set for a clash of the Titans,' says Mike Breckon. 'The late 1950s had seen dramatic drops in profits for Raleigh [and] in 1960 TI made its move on Nottingham. After more than 70 years operating as an independent company, Raleigh became part of the TI giant, with two of TI's board of directors, including the BCC managing director, placed on the Raleigh board ... There is little doubt that the TI–Raleigh merger hastened the demise of the British cycle component industry.'

Breckon, in his biography of the components millionaire Ron Kitching, quotes him as saying: 'The components manufacturers were faced with a dictator. TI–Raleigh could more or less turn round and say, "Look, if you won't let us have it at that price, we won't buy it from you." If a company couldn't exist on that price, what could they do? When you get a company like Dunlop saying they would stop manufacturing cycle tyres rather than go crawling to TI–Raleigh, it gives an idea of what it was like.'

Raleigh concentrated on everyday bikes for the everyday rider. The race market was too small for a firm of that size and it gave the work to Carlton Cycles, the company run by Gerald and Kevin O'Donovan. It was Carlton that got the call to meet Lord Plowden, the chairman and later president of Tube Investments, when fog had diverted him to one airport and TI's bigwigs had gone to another.

The O'Donovan brothers, sons of an Irish motorbike-maker and racer, collected his lordship – Edwin Noel Plowden GBE, KCB, Britain's wartime head of aircraft production, and created Baron Plowden in 1959 – and took him to their factory.

'I think he was a bit taken aback to have his hand shaken by oily palms, to be chatted up by smiling workers and to be asked for his autograph,' Gerald O'Donovan recalled. 'My lads made the most of having a live lord to themselves and I wasn't above taking advantage of it myself.' Neither man knew it but that was the start of the TI–Raleigh racing team.

The O'Donovans had been on the side of the NCU in the civil war but were bewitched into compromising their principles. Gerald O'Donovan recalled: 'I fell under the spell of a young man, Tom Simpson, who not only was a gifted track rider and time-triallist but also rode these road-races. Despite his aversion to the road-racing scene, it was Kevin who helped to find ways of sending Tom to the European scene.'

The end of the civil war between the NCU and BLRC cleared the way for Carlton, which was still under the Simpson spell. It meant the company was open to an idea from a Sheffield enthusiast called George Shaw. In 1964 he suggested the O'Donovans run an independent team in Britain. Kevin O'Donovan agreed. He called his lordship, recalled their meeting that fog-filled day, and told him Shaw's ideas. It was a successful call. Gerald O'Donovan said: 'He gave us a private subvention from TI funds, loaned us cars and drivers for European trips, and other kindness. In later years, with the pro team, he also loaned us his prop-jet.'

The domestic team worked well and Carlton even had an arrangement with *Cycling* that it would take an advertisement on the front page of the magazine every time a Carlton rider won a race. And that's how things could have stayed had Britain not entered the European Common Market. In 1976 Raleigh wanted to expand into a far bigger market and that meant a team of appeal to more than just British enthusiasts. The time had come to run a real team. O'Donovan was called on to help.

'David Duffield [later a commentator with Eurosport but then working for Raleigh] and I were told by the Chairman to get ourselves to Barcelona for the World Championship road-race,' he said. 'We were to suss out what management material might be available. We decided on Raleigh Amsterdam as the forward base, with Peter Post as team manager. George Shaw was to [continue to] look after the UK end and UK-based riders.'

Post was a good rider but his business ventures hadn't been startling. Or rather, they had: his bowling alley in Amstelveen had caught fire and failed. O'Donovan said he was no good at budgets until Raleigh's advertising manager, Sidney Woods, taught him how to do it. The disciple then became the maestro. 'Riders even needed a receipt in triplicate if they bought a bottle of Coke on expenses,' O'Donovan said. Such was the discipline that riders changed TI–Raleigh's abbreviation of TI–R Group to *Tirgruppe*, which meant firing squad.

The first team was registered in Britain and, under the rules of the time, had to have British riders. But one by one they came home – Brian Jolly, Dave Lloyd, Phil Bayton, Bob Carey – with tales bitter or discreet about getting the worst bikes, being used as cannon-fodder, metaphorically kicked because they weren't Dutch. Lloyd recalled: 'Post mellowed later but he was a swine to the British riders. He always made sure the team had the best food and stayed in the best rooms, but he certainly had a down on the British. I was always last on the massage table.'

O'Donovan said:

I will confess that in the beginning even I thought that there was some Dutch chauvinism in this. The truth was that few British riders thrive off their own island and there were certainly far too few to make up the major team we needed. We registered in Holland in 1975.

More than once Peter let riders leave who had an inflated view of their own worth, rather than spoil the balance of the rest of the team. Usually these riders learned that without the depth of team support, life was not easy. I remember him telling one Australian rider: 'You want me to pay you nice Australian tennis money? You go play tennis.'

From 1976 to 1983 Post and Raleigh amassed two world road championships (Gerrie Knetemann 1978, Jan Raas 1979), the 1980 Tour de France (Joop Zoetemelk), the Amstel Gold Race in 1978, 1979 and 1980, the Tour of Flanders in 1979 and Ghent–Wevelgem in 1980. Plus 15 world championships, five World Cups, 77 Tour stages, the Giro d'Italia, 37 Classics and 55 national championships. The French magazine *Vélo* named it top team in history and said it 'imposed its astonishing collective force from the moment the team was created', adding that Post 'maintained great cohesion in a team rich with individual strengths'.

Well, history turns circles and TI–Raleigh, which had so ruthlessly taken over the bike industry in Britain, found its team taken away in turn. It worked with a list of subsidiary sponsors of which the last, Panasonic, took over.

'We became Panasonic–Raleigh and finally the ante was so high that we moved out. We just could not meet the cost of their sort of budget,' O'Donovan said. The team folded in 1983 after 12 years.

Twelve years later many of the riders returned to a party, *Raleigh Reunie 1995*, to celebrate.

Of the rest, Lord Plowden retired as president of the TI Group in 1990. Gerald O'Donovan died at home in 2001 after a heart attack. George Shaw was connected with Carlton and Raleigh for 23 years and still works in the trade. He left Raleigh in 1989 after what Gerald O'Donovan described as internal politics. He was replaced by Paul Sherwen, a former Tour rider. Tom Simpson died in the Tour de France in 1967. Peter Post is retired in central Holland. And Raleigh? Its factory was sold machine by machine in December 1999, 109 years after it started. An era passed.

The irony is that many think of Raleigh as a British team. It never was. It had some talented and hardworking Britons, some of whom like Bob Carey went to evening classes to learn Dutch before joining. But that was little more than one year in twelve. Derek Buttle's Hercules team lasted three years and was always entirely British. That's the irony: that the better British sponsorship became, the less it went on British riders. The last attempt to field a Tour de France team was the fall-apart ANC–Halfords in 1987, which was in mayhem long before the race ended. And only some of the team were British.

Is there something in the theory that, as O'Donovan said, few British riders thrive off their own island? Let's look at that again later.

14

THE UNKNOWN HERO

The *Daily Herald* spoke of 'Booty the incomparable ... The indomitable.' There were more stories elsewhere, like 'Rider crashes four-hour barrier' in the *News Chronicle*. But compared to what cyclists thought of Ray Booty's remarkable ride in the Bath Road '100' in 1956, the reports were no more than space-fillers.

The papers had cycling correspondents, they had filed a decent story, and they were found space. But hope of more had been killed years before, when the RTTC ruled that time-trialling was best conducted in secret. Who could blame editors when the sport itself was terrified people could turn up to watch?

Front pages had been cleared when Roger Bannister broke four minutes for the mile, two years earlier. Journalists knew about running; they knew Bannister; and there were TV cameras at Iffley ready for the attempt. But papers which couldn't be told a bike race was on, still less who was riding and whether he could break a record, could scarcely be blamed for being unbothered when the first man broke four hours for 100 miles out and home.

Booty, like Bannister, was a tall and slightly goofy-looking man, his round glasses suggesting a boffin drawn blinking into daylight. He came from the East Midlands, where he belonged to the Ericsson Wheelers, and he dominated 100-mile time-trialling in the 1950s. He won the 100-mile championship every year from 1955 to 1959, a sequence equalled by only Ian Cammish between 1985 and 1989.

The build-up to a sub-four '100' followed the same tantalising steps as the four-minute mile. The difference was that while runners other than Bannister could have run the mile, Booty was the only man for 100 miles on a bike. Booty broke the 100-mile record in the 1956 national championship, but at 4:1:52 he was still two minutes adrift of a sub-four. The next big race was the Bath Road '100' on August Bank Holiday, 6 August, 1956, run in the Thames valley west of Reading, from Theale to Pangbourne, Wallingford,

Shillingford, Abingdon, then back and along the A4 to Marlborough before retracing to where it had started. It was expected to be a championship revenge for those he had beaten and, because of the needle, a spur for Booty. And sure enough he wheeled his Raleigh and its 84-inch gear to the start in Pangbourne Lane and rode it back again under heavy clouds just before 10 a.m. in 3:58:28.

The writer Byron Rogers said: 'For the 90-odd riders who set out, their abiding memory afterwards was of being passed, one, incredulously, on a hill, another on the last turn when he realised, to his horror, that the tall figure with the shock of wild hair and the protruding teeth who had started so much later, was eight minutes up on him and accelerating. The great Stan Brittain, who later turned professional, was second that day – but twelve minutes behind. Brittain said only that he would never speak again to a man who could do something like that.'

Booty himself resigned himself to an uncomfortable ride on wet roads but ended up riding faster than he expected because he wanted to catch his touring friend, Jim Ogden, and because for five miles he was trying to dominate Vin Denson, the future Tour de France rider.

He said: 'The ride up to the top turn [72 miles] seemed reasonably easy, and a glance at my watch told me I was still doing 25mph, but I remembered a similar situation last year when I took a bad packet on the return journey. However this time I felt much more comfortable and on reaching Newbury I gave it everything I had left, realising it was now or never – for this year at least.'

The simplicity of the era is demonstrated by two facts: Booty had cycled 100 miles from Nottingham to Reading the day before the race and spent 50p on bed-and-breakfast; not having a car, he scrounged a lift home as far as Nuneaton and, 100 miles at more than 25 mph in his legs, cycled the rest of the way from there.

All he has from his achievement is a medal given to him by *Cycling*, a handful of cuttings and what Rogers referred to as 'certificates of the sort schoolchildren get for religious proficiency'.

The following month Booty broke the straight-out record, a one-way ride allowed by the Road Records Association. His 3:28:40 stood for 34 years before it, too, was beaten by Cammish.

Ray Booty, after the first sub-four hour '100'

There was speculation that Booty, because he always rode a Raleigh, had more help from Nottingham than an amateur was allowed. It hardly showed. Mike Daniell, who covered the RRA attempt, took the bike for a ride. He said it was 'a battered red', which hardly suggests a pampered amateur. It was also, he said, 'of gate-like proportion surmounted by one of the longest seat pins I had ever seen. Although nearly six feet tall myself, it was all I could do to straddle the crossbar and claw the pedals round'. The record ended not with a tracksuit, a flurry of attendants and a seat in a team car but in a borrowed raincoat with a mug of tea.

Booty won the BBAR three times, won the 1958 Empire Games road-race and showed he could ride mountains as well when he won the Manx International. Ron Kitching summed him up as 'an iron man', but suggested that perhaps he 'lacked the dedication to make bike-racing a full-time career'.

Maybe he didn't want to, but he certainly had most of the qualities. What he really needed was to be part of a good continental racing team. Then I think he would have gone to the top. But whether his personality would have got in the way, that's another thing. You need a bit of modesty and humility to achieve that. It's not like being over here, where a good bike rider can dominate for a few years. Many good professionals have to go an entire season without a win. But I'm not sure if someone like the Boot could have dealt with that.

The next target was 500 miles in 24 hours. To ride for 24 hours is an achievement in itself, especially without stopping, but to beat 500 miles would be magical. When the Yorkshireman Roy Cromack did it in midsummer 1969, with 507 miles and no decimals, the record stood for a quarter of a century. When it had been his for 20 years, he told me: 'It's getting on my wick, to be honest. You know, as the years go by. I don't believe it's that good a record. It's stood for that long because nobody of any class has had a go or had the right conditions.'

By then, leaving aside the war years, Cromack had held the record three and a half times as long as anyone else. I confess that when he broke it, I was far more interested in the professional road-race championship, which had been held the same day. I watched Bill Lawrie come past Dave Nie, whose tyres were sinking in the melted road, to win the title outside Aylesbury. I had no eyes and little interest in 24-hour time-trialling and I couldn't understand why Ken Evans, the editor of *Cycling*, gave Cromack the higher billing. It took some time, as it did for many people, for the sheer size of the achievement to sink in. The ride was the only '24' that Cromack had ridden and remains the only one he ever did ride.

It was something for my dad. My dad was a professional cricketer and I always used to hero-worship him, and it gave him something to hero-worship about me. That sounds daft, I know, but I remember we drove back to Yorkshire afterwards and we stopped in a pub for a pint, and he was trying to tell somebody and they weren't interested. You know, he was absolutely chuffed to nappybreaks about it all. In fact, I think he was more excited than I was.

I suppose the 500 was an obvious target. It was a bit like Ray Booty's four-hour '100', although I wouldn't put it in the same category as that. A '100' is a lot more competitive than a '24', purely from the number of events there are and the number of people who ride "100s". But that was part of it. I reckoned I could break comp record and I wanted my name in the record books, I suppose.

Not that he was unknown to the record books, of course. He had won the '12' championship in 1967, ridden the Peace Race and the Olympic team time-trial, and he shook hands with Jacques Anquetil when he presented his trophy for the national track 10-mile championship. He is, by my reckoning, the only man to have won medals at every RTTC championship distance.

The '24' record had belonged to a red-faced farmer called Nim Carline, a man who shuffled rather than walked and barely looked the athlete that he was. The idea of beating it came up at a Clifton CC dinner and things moved from there. 'I reckoned I was basically faster than Nim, and I reckoned Nim had got it wrong anyway. He used to blast off and do 262 miles in the first 12 hours and about 220 in the second, and I didn't reckon that was the way to ride. My formula [and here he betrays his background as a maths teacher]... Well, my schedule, was 258 and 243, and I did 259.5 and 247.5, so I think it worked out the way I planned it, more or less.'

With massive understatement, he added: 'It went remarkably well, you know, for a first attempt.'

The twist is that six weeks after he broke the record, he joined the RAF. Marching up and down hurt his legs much more than cycling had ever done. He took what the RAF had taught him and moved to Shrewsbury, where he lectured in computing and went out riding with the CTC. Later he moved back to York, where he lives now in good health but with a heart pacemaker. 'I think the efforts I made when I was racing were more than my heart could take,' he said. 'When you know your body as well as a racing cyclist knows it, you can take it right to the limit, and too many years of doing that have taken their toll.'

The '24' was never part of the British Best All-rounder competition, nor the '25'. The first was thought too extreme and the second too girlie. There was a lot of credit and prestige to both but neither represented, thought the founders of the competition in April 1930, the core of proper time-trialling.

At first *Cycling* put up a 25-guinea trophy to be held permanently by the winner. Guineas – a pound and a shilling – were prices much in favour with lawyers, jewellers, dressmakers and others before decimalisation did away with such affected nonsense. Twenty-five guineas was £26. 25, a huge sum in 1930. The winning team also got a trophy but was expected to give it back.

In time the overall winner's trophy also had to be given back, which meant riders could no longer do what they wanted with it. Until then it was common for the hard-up or simply mercenary to sell their trophies. The trophy held for a year for winning the BBAR, the greatest award the sport offered for decades, was big enough and glorious enough to match the honour. It was with some alarm, therefore, that officials found one winner using it to help his children make sandcastles.

There have been many suggestions of ways to change the competition. Insisting on the average of each rider's best speed at 50 and 100 miles and 12 hours drags the sport on to traffic-filled roads which the founders could never have imagined. The quiet Sunday mornings that Ray Booty knew, hissing on tight tyres through sleeping villages and past astonished newspaper boys, have gone. Officials no longer stand in the middle of main roads to indicate where riders should turn, unworried about being hacked down by cars and lorries.

Roads are now busy both day and night. But that only made things worse as riders began enjoying and then exploiting the push and suck of passing cars and, especially, lorries. They sought out roads which any other rider would avoid and raced into roundabouts without braking, gambling that drivers who had right of way would brake in alarm and let them pass.

Those roads had slip roads to and from junctions and those proved especially dangerous. Drivers clipped riders as they drove on or off the road. Other riders plunged into the back of parked cars and for years the RTTC had to run a campaign for riders to watch where they were going. There are more deaths in time-trialling than in the apparently more dangerous sport of road-racing.

Simplicity, however, has appeal. Local officials have banned some courses at some times of day, which has had limited effect. Clubs have combined to run races only on the sort of country lane that the old-timers knew, courses they called 'sporting' and which had hills and bends. Take the importance of the course out of the race and times become relevant only to that race, say the proponents. Riders on one course and in one load of weather are no longer riding theoretical races against riders at the other end of the country.

Officials have acknowledged all these points but, as Bernard Thompson said: 'Most of the alternative systems created extra complications in a system that has proved relatively simple to operate and record from an administrative point of view.'

If a way could be found to do it, the true best all-rounder would be not a rider good at one time-trial distance and almost as good at two others but someone who could do that and ride a good road-race and perform at international level on the track. Such riders have been very few. Cromack could have done it, with his Peace Race ride and his Olympic track-riding, but not all in the same year.

The nearest that's come to it so far was in 1966, when another Yorkshireman, Arthur Metcalfe, won both the National Road-Race Championship and the BBAR. It had never been done before and it has never been done since. Ron Kitching said: 'Arthur was a real tough rider. In the Milk Race in the mid-sixties his lone breakaways in the mountain stages were legendary.'

Metcalfe, apart from attracting Les West's enmity because of personality differences – something the unflappable Metcalfe noticed less than West – was one of the first sponsored amateurs.

The pioneering sponsored club was Romford, where the royal blue jerseys had the name of the Duomatic washing machine on them for two years. Only nominated riders could wear advertising and Metcalfe's club, Leeds St Christopher, put its named members into different colours: white with an orange band, embroidered with the name of the Leeds cycle dealer, Bob Jackson.

Metcalfe had won the Milk Race two years earlier and in 1966 was feeling 'in a bit of a rut'. And so he won the BBAR, almost as an afterthought:

> I remember thinking that I needed a change: I wasn't going well. I'd ridden some time-trials when I was 19 or 20, when I started cycling, because the funny thing then was that I was scared of descending, especially in a bunch.
>
> I didn't start cycling until I was well into my teens and then I lost a couple of years in the army. I'd started cycling then and I can remember riding from north of London up to Norfolk to ride a race, and only having an apple or something to eat on the way. And when I got there I hadn't got enough to stay anywhere so I asked at the police station if I could sleep in the cells, but they wouldn't let me. In the end I found someone who asked how much money I had and said she'd put me up for that.
>
> Anyway, I was in a mixed [activity] club and like all the lads I'd ridden a few time-trials in the past, so I thought I'd have another go.

There was no idea then that he'd try for the BBAR, only that he'd have a break from road-racing. He entered a '50' at Catterick and turned up at the start slightly hazy about what he expected of himself. 'I wasn't sure about it, to tell you the truth, so I ambled round. After the first half I was as fresh as a daisy and I wished I'd gone harder.' He came second in 1:56, which is what comes of 'ambling round'. 'Oh, there's a bit of potential there,' he thought. 'I'll have another go.' And so he entered a '100' at Newark and won in 4:10 in a gale which saw a lot of the field climbing off. 'I was quite pleased that I'd beaten a lot of the testing lads in that race. Happy memories I've got of that. A real stinking day. And when I thought of what I'd done, it was then that the idea of the BBAR cropped up, I think. I'd beaten everyone else in a time-trial.'

He rode a '50' in 1:52 and then a '100' in 3:56. His memory is that he was the fourth in history to beat four hours; by Bernard Thompson's calculation, he was fifth, but at any rate fourth after Ray Booty. All he needed was a '12', but he said the national championship organisers wouldn't let him ride because he didn't have a qualifying time. Instead, he drove to East Anglia, fresher and more experienced than his first ride there, to ride the last event available to him.

Those who chuckled at an upstart roadman trying to barge into national championship ended their day with a surprise; Metcalfe finished only half a mile outside competition record, wishing he'd gone a little harder. 'It was pitch dark at the start,' he remembered, taken aback after years of starting his races after lunch. 'It was bitterly cold and I started in my tracksuit top.' And so, almost by chance and mainly because he had the fidgets, Metcalfe won the BBAR in 22.576 mph. And despite two rides in the Tour de France, despite his road championship and his Milk Race, it stayed his sweetest memory until he died of cancer at 64 in 2002.

> You get a wonderful feeling of elation when you win something like that, and winning the Milk Race was wonderful, too, but it's a gradual realisation as you hold the jersey. And the BBAR is also a more gradual realisation, it's something that builds up for you. But what you've got to remember is that they were victories, whereas the Tour de France was an experience.

I went to the BBAR concert that year because I had friends in Metcalfe's club. I had a sense of history having been created in a small way. Metcalfe remembered: 'I didn't speak to any of the die-hards [of time-trialling] but I got a very nice reception from everyone. It means a lot to me, that, and I don't think anybody had done it before or since, not even in different years. Phil Griffiths came close when he came second in the road, but...' As I wrote of Metcalfe at the time: 'He didn't complete the sentence. What he means is that he's the one and only.'

Arthur Metcalfe (winner of the Milk Race in 1964)
before the start of the 1965 race at Brighton

15

SIXTY MINUTES OF SIXTY SECONDS

To a 25-mile specialist, a '12' or a '24' must seem like pole-squatting. In fact it took some time for the '25' to be seen as a worthy and not just a warm-up distance, the position that the 10-mile still holds now. It was only when the target of being back at the finish within an hour became feasible but not yet touchable that the event got its glamour.

As with so many barriers, the 60-minute '25' was approached and then seemed irreducible. But once it had been broken, just as with the four-minute mile in running, it fell over and over.

The history is muddled. The first rider to manage 25 miles in less than an hour was the Irishman Alo Donegan, from Portarlington, and a member of the Irish Road Club. In 1934 he rode 59:05 to win the Palmer Trophy '25' run by the Harp Club. He had the luxury, unlike British riders, of being able to wear shorts. And it has to be said that many who heard the news in Britain were frankly sceptical, not least because it had happened in Ireland, still considered then a vaguely comical country where a mile may well not be a mile.

But Donegan had undeniably robbed the British of their prize. A week later he broke the 50-mile record with 2:3:57 and a year later he again went under the hour for a '25'. Pictures of him on the track show a lean greyhound of a man, obviously strong and surprisingly modern in appearance for the era.

The '25' record had suddenly become a foreign record. The British, who had started time-trialling and lent it to the colonies and former colonies, were making the discovery that footballers and rugby players were to make a couple of decades later: that they could be upended by the nations they once looked on with a patronising smile. Ireland certainly seemed to be where the magic lay, even if it was only in not having to wear black from neck to toe and carry a bell. Ireland was where the stylish George Fleming went in 1938, borrowing a pair of wheels and tagging on to the end of a '25' in what was known then as a 'private' – a timed performance not considered part of the main race. It had been bad enough to hear of Donegan's 59:05; that Fleming could go to this same pixies' island and ride 57:56 was simply greeted with disbelief.

Now, not just once but twice the record had been beaten in Ireland. The prestige of being the first to ride under the hour in Britain – simply under the hour, remember – had been grossly lessened. Fleming could have done it and simply added to his prestige, but it didn't happen quickly enough. He was beaten to it by Ralph Dougherty, whom reporters began to call the Rugby Flyer for his home town and the club he had joined in the early 1930s (although result sheets attach him to Leamington C & AC). 'He rapidly became the fastest rider, head and shoulders above everyone else,' says the Rugby RCC's history.

Dougherty won the Solihull Invitation race in 1939 with 59:29. The times, literally, had started to change though because he wasn't alone; just more than a quarter of an hour later a second rider, George Nightingale, also finished in less than an hour. In 59:37, in fact.

Dougherty's odder contribution to cycling history is to have been disciplined for his socks. Unlike Donegan, he and the other British riders had had to dress wholly in black and compete in secret. Dougherty astonished officials in 1944, and risked world order by wearing white or at any rate 'light-coloured' socks over his tights. He had turned up at the Birchfield '25' and asked to set off at the end in a private ride, as Fleming had in Ireland. The arrangement meant he wasn't in the running for first place or a prize – that wasn't disputed. What was disputed was his right to ride in anything but a black jacket and tights … and he was disqualified from an event he hadn't actually been riding.

That rule, by the way, clung on towards the end of the war. It would have gone in the end because it had become unnecessary, outmoded and, frankly, ridiculous. What did for it in the end was rationing. There was too little material to go round for clothing and it became not only difficult but un-British to insist on tights. They disappeared and were never mourned.

'Today,' says Bernard Thompson in *Alpaca to Skin Suit*, his history of the RTTC, 'all this seems nonsensical and contradictory. On the one hand the sport's administrators were concerned with the safety of time-triallists sharing the public highways with other motor traffic and on the other seeking to shroud the sport in secrecy to a point where each competitor was required to wear "dark and inconspicuous clothing". In the best interests of safety when time-trialling on busy roads in modern times, competitors seek to make themselves as conspicuous as possible.' They are even, he says, compelled to wear fluorescent or reflective numbers, something which would have horrified Freddie Bidlake and his successors – as would any sort of acknowledgement that a race was going on.

More than uniforms changed with the war. Before then, and for a while afterwards, riders preferred fixed wheels and tiny frames, perhaps with wooden rims but certainly with tyres that modern riders would use in a cyclo-cross. Time-triallists viewed derailleurs in the way that early Tour de France riders had seen them, although for very much longer. They considered the few that they'd seen – precious few made it across from the Continent – as unreliable, which they sometimes were. They also thought them heavy and almost girlie.

They twiddled – or span, as Americans say – all through the winter and sometimes on training rides that went on for 200 miles or more. When Ken Joy rode 180 miles to see his girlfriend in Nottingham, he said that even then long rides were 'the only way I knew of getting fit'. The season started at Easter with so-called middle-gear events, in which riders' gear size was limited. They then moved to higher gears in races as the weather improved, always anxious not to push too hard and acquire a condition known at the time as 'Easter knees'.

Riders took pride in how fast they could pedal. In 1955 Ron Jowers turned a single 90-inch gear to record 26.667 mph for a '30'. It was faster than the '25' record. There is no such thing as a limit to human performance – in 1980 Tony Doyle rode at 124 rpm for 56:30 to win the Crabwood '25' in February 1980 – but legs can go only so fast for so long. There is a practical limit to a single gear on a course that is neither flat nor protected from the wind.

The change came in 1961 when John Woodburn won the '25' championship on a derailleur. He used a single chainring of 52 and a five-speed block of 14–18 to finish in 56:01. Traditionalists were appalled at the way he heaved at his gears instead of turning them like Jowers. But results told. Gears grew larger and pedalling speeds slower until, says the coach Ramin Minovi: 'Many of the prolific winners of the 1960s were weightlifters on bicycles.'

Few went as fast as they hoped. Some went very fast indeed. Alf Engers' entry in the *Golden Book of Cycling*, dated 23 November 1991, says:

For twenty years the name of Alf Engers was synonymous with 25 miles time-trials. He dominated the short-distance scene in such a fashion that he was known as King Alf. Engers' name on a start card was sure to guarantee a big crowd at the finish in a shower of nervous anticipation of what he would achieve. Engers could have been a first-class road or trackman. Indeed, he dabbled with success at both, but it was his talent, dedication, and showmanship that saw him take 25-miling into unknown territory.

He first broke competition record in 1959, recording 55 minutes 11 seconds. In 1969 he took the first of his six national championships, winning in 54 minutes 42 seconds, and later breaking competition record first with a time of 51 minutes 59 seconds and then improving his own figures to 51 minutes to raise speculation about an inside 50 minutes time for the distance.

Engers claimed his second national title in 1972 and then followed an unbeaten sequence to 1976. Yet the best was still to come.

In the first week in August 1978, a startled clubworld heard the news that on the E72, first Eddie Adkins, then Engers, had broken competition record in the Unity CC 25. Adkins recorded 50 minutes 50 seconds and then eight minutes later, Engers finished with an incredible 49 minutes 24 seconds. The seemingly unattainable had been achieved.

The record stood for 13 years, such was the measure of the man and his ride.

Bernard Thompson says of it: 'It was a glorious moment but overshadowed somewhat by subsequent complaints about Engers' riding in the centre of the road. There was an inquiry and eventually the record was ratified.'

The fun of Engers is that he was anything but the bone-headed, introverted and obsessed stereotype – a false stereotype, it has to be said – that many roadmen have of time-triallists. Few riders were quite as full of mischief. Engers waged a perpetual war against the RTTC and in particular with one of its national officials, an amiable chap called Ted Kings who looked the water-board clerk that he was. The height of the tussle came in the flower-power era of the 1970s. Engers was always a colourful dresser, although never a hippie, but he excelled himself when it came to an interview in *Cycling*. Knowing how it would upset Kings, he insisted on being pictured not only in a kaftan but sitting cross-legged on a dustbin. 'I don't know why I did it,' he said. 'But I knew the effect it would have.'

The funny thing is that just as Arthur Metcalfe was never that bothered about Les West, so Kings was quietly amused at Engers. Not approving, of course, but slowly smiling in a 'boys will be boys' way.

Engers exerted a presidential superiority over short-distance time-trialling. Lesser riders all but paid obeisance. Knowing they couldn't match him, they settled for imitation. When Engers said once that his concentration before a race compelled him to acknowledge others only with a nod and a grunt, aspirants and no-hopers alike would try the same before collapsing in giggles.

Alf Engers

He came out with quotable quotes. His predecessor at the top, Trevor Morgan, had spoken of a 'sea of darkness' that overcame him in full effort (leading riders all over the country to see whether they could manage it themselves, if only to know what he had been talking about). Engers matched that in 1969 with: 'There are many times… when physically I would welcome a car hitting me and cutting it all short there and then, I hurt so much.'

In a sport already conscious of the dangers that riders faced on fast dual-carriageways, and coming from a rider often accused of riding far out in the road to take advantage of the vacuum of passing traffic, it was a remark guaranteed to attract attention. The charm of Engers was that there was none of the nastiness that would have made similar antics distasteful from less charismatic and charming riders. And little of the big-headedness. Engers remained until the end of his career an imp with a huge sense of his own mischief and a talent that comes only once a decade, if that.

If riders like Engers couldn't imagine a '12', imagine their reaction at the longest records of all.

Two policemen from Leeds, names now lost, are said to be the first people to have ridden from Land's End to John o'Groats. Modern riders do about 870 miles – they're free to take any route. But today's bridges weren't there in 1882 and they had to take – and wait for – ferries as well as bumping along unmade roads on penny-farthings. It took them 14 days.

The first formal attempt was by George Mills, the Bordeaux–Paris winner, in July 1886 when he was 19. His time, on a 52-inch penny-farthing, was 5 days 1 hour and 45 minutes. The record still stands.

The first man in less than three days was Tom Peck in 1908. He took two days 22 hours and 42 minutes, or more than six hours better than what went before. It included two crashes in the Highlands. His record lasted only a few days, when the wind turned and pushed Harry Green from one end of the country to the other in 2:19:50. He also crashed, not in the Highlands but while trying to warn his followers of a flock of sheep he'd encountered in Devon.

The record stood for 21 years, beaten in 1929 by the Raleigh professional, Jack Rossiter, who rode in continuous rain for 36 hours.

'It seemed like the end of the world,' he said, but he nevertheless pushed on and reached the north of Scotland in 2:13:22.

The record went under two days in 1965, to a paid-up member of a sex club. That, at any rate, was Richard William Ewart Poole's joke: he claimed the MIDDLESEX ROAD CLUB across his tracksuit top divided at the zip so that one half read SEX CLUB. His 1:23:46:35 made history – and ended in black tragedy.

Dick Poole set off from Land's End at 9.45 a.m. on Wednesday, 16 June, wearing his club jersey, white socks pulled to mid-calf, his front light on the left rather than the conventional right fork. He was 31 and experienced instantly what Ken Joy described as 'the very lonely moment of being wished goodbye at Land's End'.

Like others, he crashed, cutting himself as he lost balance at roadworks near Cullompton. He got snarled up in traffic at Wellington. He lost ten minutes on Reg Randall's existing record of 2:10:40. A further six minutes disappeared as the cuts began to hurt towards Bristol. By Gloucester the deficit was half an hour. The organiser, Bernard Thompson, told me once that: 'Nothing is more miserable, more deflating, than a record attempt that fails; nobody says anything, nobody smiles; the whole thing has been done in vain.' He must have feared that then.

Percy Stallard, David Duffield and the cartoonist Johnny Helms appeared to urge Poole through the night. The rain fell, battery lights refused to stay alight, clothing became sodden. Effective waterproofs had yet to be invented. So, too, had modern clothing and Poole rode in a nylon anorak and a sweater of patterned wool. The deficit reached 49 minutes after 320 miles, at Whitchurch.

Helpers weren't allowed to pass riders for fear they might pace them. They were powerless, therefore, to keep Poole on the right route at Lancaster and only a local official saved him when he spotted Poole and pointed him the way he should have gone.

The first 24 hours passed north of Penrith, where Poole had ridden 454 miles to Randall's 459.5. He slipped ahead for the first time from the border and by Stirling his smooth pedalling began to gain on the punching style of little Randall. He was within two minutes of his own schedule.

He complained of feeling sleepy and stopped several times for food and to have his dressings changed. But then, elated that it had all nearly ended, he rode the hilly 18 miles of Struie at 17 mph. It was the best part of the ride: 'It was marvellous. The rabbits and squirrels running over the roads, the occasional deer and the cloudless, new-born day. It made me feel good and I knew then that I would do it.'

He reached Wick (855 miles) with ten minutes in hand and, in anorak and cap, passed the timekeepers at John o'Groats in 1:23:46:35 after 871.7 miles. He'd got through four club jerseys, two pairs of shorts, two pairs of shoes, several pairs of socks, a gallon of rice and fruit salad, seven pints of Complan, 12 oranges, eight pints of coffee, 13 pints of tea and eight pints of Ribena.

'I was in the state you'd expect after the end-to-end,' he said. 'But they started saying I should go for the 1,000 miles. I didn't want to but they were saying it was only another 120 miles and I'd barely have to do it at club run speed. So I agreed and I had a rest and I set off again.'

That was where things went wrong, although nobody realised it. There were, to be exact, 128.3 miles, a sixth of the original distance. He needed to ride at 13 mph. And he did it easily. He took a 30-minute break, set off at 20 mph for 45 minutes, dropped to 17 mph, then struggled on through hail and wind. Thompson, following in his van, watched the milometer. From just before the 128.3 miles he and the timekeeper began noting landmarks every mile and clocked when Poole passed. They did the same for the next 10 miles and then called Poole to a halt. He had got that far in 2:8:6, more than two and a half hours better than Randall. Exactly where the 1,000 miles had passed could be calculated when the route was measured. The intermediate times of the mile on each side of the 1,000 could be averaged, as they would be on the finishing circuit of '12' or '24', and the result defined.

The problem came with 'when the route was measured'. The exact distance from Land's End to John o'Groats didn't matter. Not for the end-to-end. Provided he started at one and finished at the other, Poole could take any route he liked. The trouble was that the whole distance, even with the extra 10 miles, didn't come to 1,000.

It was yards short. Poole *would* have broken the record had he ridden 1,000 miles but the truth was that he hadn't.

'We couldn't understand it,' he said. 'They measured it again and then the motoring organisations joined in and they measured it and still it came out short. And it was getting to be quite a story in the papers. It took a lot of puzzling to work out what had happened. We had based our attempt on the schedule that Reg Randall used. The route was clear except in Scotland, where there was a choice between going straight over a mountain, which was the shorter route, or round it, which was longer but meant he could ride faster.

'We didn't know which way he'd gone but we assumed the shorter way, and that's the way I went. The over-the-mountain route was 10 miles and so many yards shorter and so I hadn't done 1,000 miles when we were all sure I'd ridden 1,010.'

Randall's 1960 record of 1,000 miles in 2:10:40 (no seconds recorded) stood for more than 40 years until Gethin Butler, a 33-year-old from Preston, left the south door of the Land's End Hotel at 10 a.m. on 27 September, 2001, to reach the front door of John o'Groats Hotel in 1:20:4:19. He then broke the 1,000-mile record in 2:7:53:7.

16

DASH FOR THE CASH

The world of professional, or at least semi-professional road-racing went on quite distinct from the sheltered waters of time-trialling and record-breaking. Lone riders against the clock had, on the face of it, no other wish than to improve their own or someone else's time. Road riders, on the other hand, dreamed of riding the Tour de France. Or, if they weren't good enough for that, of paying their expenses.

There always had been professionals in cycling even if right at the start nobody thought to call them that. It was the growth of the Olympic Games and their strict amateur principles – principles which the British adopted so enthusiastically that at one time they tried to pick only those with a private income to take part – which forced a distinction between pro and amateur.

Now, if you insisted that amateurs could win no money at all while allowing professionals to earn as much as they could, there was always a chance that the professionals would move further and further ahead while the amateurs stayed where they were. People who were allowed to pocket nothing could hardly be encouraged by offering them twice nothing. Professionals, on the other hand, could be and were offered more and more. And each time the level of pro racing increased, the greater the gap became over the amateurs.

In particular, the gap increased because the biggest races got longer. It was all very well taking five days off work to ride Brighton–Glasgow but a month to ride the Tour de France was different, especially given all the races that would have to be ridden to get to that standard. It was that gap, you'll remember, that led to the creation of a category midway between professional and amateur. Independents were apprentice professionals. They could wear advertising and accept money in wages and prizes and yet they weren't full professionals. The idea was that a few years in this middle class would give them the strength and courage to turn fully professional or make them realise they had no future and go back to being amateurs.

In fact, little of that sort happened. Some did turn professional and some became very good. But most stayed where they were and – on the European mainland, anyway – raced against those professionals who weren't good enough to ride the Classics and stage races and stayed behind to ride round-the-houses races.

Those town-centre racers soon realised they didn't have to turn professional to take part. They could ride just as well against professionals if they stayed as independents. They could ride the same races as the professionals and win the same money and a lot more sponsors were willing to hand over a bike and a jersey to an independent than pay a decent wage to a professional. And when there were no professional races to ride, independents could compete against amateurs and, in theory at any rate, outclass them.

The independent class became a gulf into which thousands were happy to settle with no intention of doing anything else. In Britain, they couldn't do anything else anyway; except in occasional years there were no professional teams to join, and when there *were* professional teams, all those pros could do was ride against independents.

These days there are many who see the old independents as romantic. They were rough, people tell you, making up with wiliness for their lack of youth. One, Trevor Fenwick, remembers a club dinner programme which only half-jokingly asked: 'Would independents please eat their sandwiches outside.'

The UCI wasn't impressed by that roughhouse romance, though, and in 1966 it gave all independents two years to turn pro or revert to amateurism. Going back to being an amateur was hard in Britain, where any rider who'd touched a pound note even as an independent had to spend two years out of the sport to purify himself. Many just packed in cycling, at least for two years. The rest turned pro, often riding for the same sponsors they had had as independents.

The new professionals were offered money, often more than the independents had earned, but still not a lot. Colin Lewis, now running a bike shop in Torquay, turned down a chance to join the AC Boulogne–Billancourt in Paris because he could get £4 a week from Mackeson, run from the London bike shop of Condor Cycles. The ACBB was a feeder for French pro teams but the certainty of £4 a week seemed preferable to just the hope of something better. That was 1967 and the paucity of Lewis's wage compared to real professionals became sharply illustrated in that year's Tour de France when his roommate, Tom Simpson, paid more for one consignment of drugs than Lewis earned on his bike all year.

To ride the Tour as a first-year pro was something even the most talented continental riders have rarely been asked to do. To finish it was astonishing. Even more remarkable was Arthur Metcalfe, whom French reporters discovered was riding the race in three weeks' holiday from work from Carlton Cycles in Nottinghamshire.

'I had a day off after I got back from Paris,' Metcalfe said, 'and then I went back to work, although they did give me some time off for training.'

Metcalfe had done all he could as an amateur the previous year by winning the BBAR and the road-race championship in the same year, having already won the Milk Race. He and his third wife, Anne, were planning to move to the south of France in 2002. We had arranged to go for rides together, Arthur promising to take things easy for me. He suggested some of the climbs he'd tackled in the Tour and spoke of his memories of those days. He thought the modern Tour should be longer – 'Tours of a proper length,' he said, 'Tours of 2,500 miles.'

To ride 90 miles a day is not the legend of the Tour de France. The philosophy of the Tour is that it's an epic of courage. The way it's going, it'll be a set of criteriums soon. We had stages of 223 kilometres. Sure, they go 2 mph faster now, but you'd expect that. And there are 70 more riders. I was working for Carlton Cycles. British riders are full-time pros now and they're better than we ever were, so they can ride further.

The argument is that they want a clean Tour. But you can ride 2,500 miles clean. The race may go 1 mph slower but from the roadside you'd never notice it. You can't see a difference that small.

I said that you may not see it but if he took me a single mile an hour too fast I knew I'd feel it. He laughed. We said we'd meet when he moved to France ... and then came a message that he was dying of cancer. He'd been for a few rides with lads he ought to have beaten and he'd struggled. A few months later he was dead.

Metcalfe's rival, Les West, turned professional for Holdsworth, a London bike shop team, and came fourth in the world road-race in 1970, the year that Porter won his second title. Of the other pros, Lewis's team-mate, Hugh Porter, won the world pursuit championship three times. The Ghent landlady Miriam Deene, who accommodated many visiting British riders in the 1960s – Barry Hoban lived there for eight years – said of Porter: 'When he was training for the Sixes, his dedication was remarkable. Every morning he would ride from Zomergem to Knokke and Sluis on the Dutch border, then to Maldegem and back here, about 100 kilometres.'

The breakthrough that would have made full-time professionals of all of them never came. There was no shortage of sponsors, for races if not teams, but few stayed more than a few years. Until there were more races, there would never be more riders. All the sport needed was two races a day, one for the stars and a smaller one elsewhere for less talented riders, just as jobbing professionals ride criteriums in Belgium while the stars ride the Classics.

Since that didn't happen, professional racing didn't look secure. Only a small number of amateurs turned professional each year. Many amateurs demanded more than any team could pay. Most teams were sponsored from within the cycle industry, more for goodwill than commercial gain. An outside sponsor, had one been found, could have paid more but that would have swept up the best riders and killed off the lesser teams, just as Hercules had.

The British Professional Cycle Racing Association put the era's yearly average at 40 riders. But that was an average, not a constant. There were sometimes little more than 20. The more the numbers fell, the less inclined the best riders were to turn professional in Britain.

Races in Britain declined as well. The big races went – the Isle of Wight three-day, the Tour of the South-west, the Vaux Grand Prix – to be replaced by what riders dismissed as barrel racing. Criteriums round city streets could be exciting but most courses were no more than barrels set several hundred metres apart on a sea front. The riders just went up and down, up and down. And they couldn't complain: they had at least a race a weekend. The trouble was that the races were put on by amateurs, from their own enthusiasm and often subsidised from their own pocket. If a bunch of ungrateful pros moaned too much, the organiser would reflect that he had put more effort into his race than his riders had and ask himself whether it was worthwhile. And another race would disappear.

There was always a feeling that good times were around the corner. One false dawn was the interest of the boxing promoter, Mike Barratt. Like others, he saw an under-financed and unexploited sport. In June 1977 he contracted Eddy Merckx, Raymond Poulidor and Luis Ocaña to ride the new cycling circuit at Temple Mills in east London. It was the biggest collection of stars since the Manx Grand Prix had attracted the likes of Jacques Anquetil, André Darrigade and Rik van Looy to the Isle of Man in the 1950s and 1960s.

Barratt liked what he'd done and put on a Tour of Britain, but rows during the race and Barratt's despair of cycling politics made him walk away from the sport. Within three years of Merckx in London and two years of a Tour of Britain, there were just three teams and 21 riders at the start of 1980. With many wry smiles from old independents, amateurs were allowed to race with professionals to make up their numbers.

But then, again, came a reprieve. A Midlands rider, Mick Morrison, attracted the interest of ANC, a transport business that carried the initials of its owner Tony Capper. Then the promoter Alan Rushton devised a series of televised criteriums and, in 1983, the Milk Race opened to professionals.

An ANC rider, Malcolm Elliott, won a series of televised criteriums in 1986 and the same year's Milk Race was won by his team-mate Joey McLoughlin, as dark-haired and dark-eyed as Elliott was blond. The successes gave Capper ambitions. He decided to field a team in the following year's Tour de France.

The trouble was, says the journalist Tony Bell, that: 'The ANC cycling team was a product of the 1980s, and was a perfect reflection of the brash, success-at-all-costs, don't-worry-about-tomorrow ethos of that decade. And just like many other successes of the period, when it came to the crunch it was underpinned by nothing more than hot air and empty bank accounts.'

In the words of *Procycling*: 'During the Tour riders suddenly discovered they were not being paid, the boss disappeared, and the squad went belly-up later in the year.' The riders, of whom only four finished, were outclassed. The management proved not up to the job. The misery was compounded – and colourfully recorded – by the presence of the sportswriter Jeff Connor, who travelled with the team to write a book but had no idea just how good the story was to be.

The bubble burst outside ANC as well as within it. The fiasco of the Tour and ANC suggested it wasn't only the team but the whole sport that was underpinned by 'nothing more than hot air'. The number of teams, riders and races fell year by year never to recover. In 2000 the UCI abandoned professionals just as it had independents and declared the sport open; no professionals, no amateurs, just bike-riders. Now there was no need to run a pro team. Sponsorship went into the growing and cheaper sport of mountain-bike racing – mountain bikes were the saviour of many a bike company and bike shop – and what was left for road-racing went to sponsored clubs that rode in bike-shop jerseys for expenses and bonuses. Just like independents, really.

All this was sad enough, but the fiasco came all over again. British racing went no further than sponsored club riders and a handful of *soi-disant* professionals who were no more than independents. Abroad, though, there were still full-scale teams and classic races and epic stage races like the Tour de France and Giro d'Italia.

It was into that field that a former motocross rider called Julian Clark hoped to break. With little experience of bike-racing beyond a few local races but with an enthusiasm and talent that many more experienced cyclists had failed to show, he persuaded the vegetarian-food company started by Linda McCartney, wife of the former Beatle Paul, to sponsor a team.

It would start with small Continental races and build up to the Tour. And things went well. The original line-up of mainly British riders was discarded, Raleigh-style, for a more international roster but the team grew stronger, to the extent that the Australian champion David McKenzie won a stage of the Giro d'Italia in 2000.

Hope, however, once more triumphed over experience in 2001. The team's launch for 2002 was to be at Trafalgar Square at the end of January. Everything had been arranged. Riders flew in from all over Europe and from Australia and checked in at the Travel Inn at Bagshot, Surrey. The next day they would go together to central London and show off their new jerseys with the names of their new sub-sponsors.

There had already been claims that riders hadn't been paid all their wages from the previous year. But that wasn't unusual in bike racing, especially in new teams still struggling to find their place. Some riders declined to be involved again but most, and officials like the team manager and former Tour yellow jersey Sean Yates, had confidence in the sums that Clark said he was negotiating.

The worries really started when Clark didn't arrive at Bagshot. He was ill, it was said, with a stress-related condition. And stress there certainly would have been. It emerged that not only was Linda McCartney no longer sponsoring the team but that nor were other names on the new jerseys. What's more, Linda McCartney was not only not the sponsor for 2002 but it hadn't been the sponsor for 2001 either. Its new owner, Heinz, hadn't wanted a bike team but it had let Clark use the name to attract other sponsors. But there was no deal and no money, neither in 2001 nor in 2002.

Then the car company Jaguar said it had talked about sponsorship but not gone ahead. Its logo should never have been used. The Australian wine company Jacob's Creek said its name, too, appeared without a proper sponsorship deal. It had been asked for backing during the Tour Down Under, it said, but all it had given was some wine and a small sum to have its trademark on the jersey. A spokesman said: 'We were surprised when we heard there was supposed to be a $1.7 million deal for the season.'

17

GOLD AT THE RAINBOW'S END

Cycling has one little touch which, so far as I know, is copied in no other big sport in the world: its world champions are identified by a jersey they wear until they are defeated in another world championship. It's a pleasant symbol, too, because the jersey is plain white with, around the chest, the so-called rainbow bands – the copyright five stripes that the UCI uses to hallmark its champions. There have been many rainbow jerseys, right down to trick cycling and bicycle polo. Some say there are far too many, that their number devalues their worth. They say, too, that some championships are inherently more prestigious than others, an opinion that the UCI went some way to supporting when it made subtle changes to the design to distinguish between champions on the road, the track and against the clock.

The most coveted of all championships, in most people's view anyway, are those on the road: in descending order, they are for professionals, for amateurs and for women. Only two British men have worn a rainbow for the road-race in the last 80 years. Their tales are as instructive as they are fascinating. Here they are, in reverse chronological order.

In the mid-1960s a rider most British enthusiasts would have thought at least improbable went off to Holland to perfect his trade on the road. Graham Webb was a gangly, slow-talking man from Birmingham, whose height – well over six feet – and strength and often mournful face reminded the more literary of the giant moron in John Steinbeck's *Of Mice and Men*.

That was my opinion of him, that he was a big thickie from Brum, all brawn and no more brain than he needed to turn each pedal in turn. It was a view I put simply in passing to Alan Gayfer, a former editor of *Cycling*. In Gayfer's characteristic explosive way, I was put straight: Webb, he said, was nobody's fool, a man of intelligence and insight and a dry sense of humour even if, he conceded, that wasn't how he first came over.

As a kid, Webb used to ride repeatedly from Birmingham to his aunt's home in Gloucester. Or, at any rate, as far along that route that he could. Gloucester more than once proved to be further than he could manage and he would fall into a roadside ditch in exhaustion – and then try again next week.

'I just enjoyed it,' he said, when I went to see him in the village near Ghent where he lives. 'I enjoyed suffering, I suppose. I still do.' When I heard him say that, and when I saw that same doom-laden face made more messianic now by a beard, I couldn't help thinking that my first conclusions weren't unreasonable.

There was the same naïve approach to his first race in Britain. He'd met a member of the Solihull club and went to its clubroom. Not unusually for a cycling club, he was ignored. Bike clubs are friendly places but not at first. Thin, gangly 16-year-olds have to force their way into the cliques, and Webb was too shy for that.

'This went on for a few weeks but no one came up to me. Then Mick Shakespeare came up one night and he said, "Are you riding the club '25'?" I said, "What's that?" He told me and I said, "Yeah, all right, what do I have to do?"'

The rules were explained and Webb turned up in a T-shirt, cut-down jeans and some plimsolls. The sight of all his club mates changing into racing gear overawed him and he stayed in the background, waiting for someone to tell him what to do next. Nobody did.

I thought, 'Bugger this' and I rode up to the start. I didn't know riders were supposed to start every minute. The timekeeper said, 'You're too late; you'll have to wait'. Well, they pushed me off and I was ten minutes late starting and I thought I had to catch all the blokes in front of me to win the race. I changed into top gear straight away on this old Hercules Harlequin and I knocked my pump off the down tube and I had to wait for the cars to come past, then turn round and pick my pump up.

I quickly caught someone and I waited for him. And he was telling me 'Clear off, clear off!' Very unsociable, I thought. I rode on and went round the turn in the road, came back, and the chain jumped off between the block and the frame. So I had to get off the bike, and I'd got a whole tool kit with me, spanner, oil can, cloth for cleaning my hands and so on, and this was wrapped round my seat tube with a spare inner tube. I had to undo the back wheel, put the chain on, do up the wheel nuts, put everything behind the seat tube and carry on.

Well, I got to the finish and I look around. Hell, what happens now? So I cleared off and went home. Anyway, Thursday night, back to the clubhouse and the same thing, just sitting in the corner looking at all these people, and one of these chaps, Graham Kelly, he came over and said, 'Is your name Graham Webb?' He said, 'That time-trial on Sunday, you had the fastest time.' I went as red as a beetroot. I'd done 1:1:31 and if I'd started on time and not had any trouble I'd have broken the hour on this old bike, maybe. So in the Solihull I was famous from that day on and everyone wanted to talk to me.

That same lugubrious innocence never left him. It irritated a lot of people and there are many who reckon Webb didn't get the breaks in national teams because of it. Equally, there are those who put it the other way round, that no team would want anyone that apparently awkward. Webb could see it for himself. He was ignored for the Olympic team and in 1966 he left for Holland, where the same physical clumsiness and simple ideals came to pay. But not before he won his last race in England, near Portsmouth, by 13 minutes.

His first Dutch race was near the Belgian border, in Breda. The weather was awful.

It was running up cobbled roads ['running', a transliteration from the Dutch that Webb speaks in everyday life, means 'the race went, …], and they were using a dirt track on the side of the road with holes you could put a whole wheel in, and they were covered with water. It was really thrilling because I had something I could dig my teeth into. I was pushing and shoving all the time, and I'd get to the back of the echelon, riding on the grass, on the road, on the cobbles, on the road – up the dykes and down them – and I was really enjoying myself.

And there was this one chap and he was really dangerous, and he kept pushing me, and I got to the back of the echelon and he was trying not to come to the front. And he was shouting *'Pas op! Pas op!'* [Watch it, mate!] all the time. I don't know if it was very sporting of me or not but I put him in the ditch, not really to get rid of him but I wanted the other riders to know I wasn't going to play around. It was only a grass ditch and I knew he wasn't going to hurt himself and after that I didn't have to push any more.

At one stage we went up this dyke. The blokes in front started to slip on the wet cobbles and mud and I was having to take the corners wider and wider, and I slipped into the grass and over the dyke and into the sea [river] – seven metres. I was covered in black mud. I dragged my bike out of the water and up the bank and I got back on and started chasing. I caught a few who'd got shot off and finished sixteenth, covered in slime and freezing cold, in my first race. Anyway, I was more or less famous for my first race in Holland. I was a hero, for being sixteenth. I couldn't understand it.

Even to try to understand that, you have to see a Dutch criterium. They are nothing like British, or even Belgian races. They are half as fast again, on circuits often only a kilometre long, and a combination of pride and combines and never-ending money prizes makes breaking into them as likely as breaking into a bank.

Those prizes often include primes for the leader each lap – every kilometre, remember – and then extra prizes for a race-long points competition based on placings each lap. In his second race in Holland, Webb faced a kilometre-long course with seven corners. Sprinters went for the intermediate prizes and Webb went with them, less to challenge them but because he couldn't yet understand Dutch well enough to understand the prize list and the loudspeaker announcements. He won the first prime and kept going. Before long he was so far ahead that the tail end of the race was just in front of him.

'I could have lapped them,' he said, 'but I wasn't sure whether I'd have to sprint again for the primes. So I just left them hanging there. I won 98 primes plus the *klassement* , the points competition.'

In one race he lapped the field three times.

'I wouldn't lap them round the back of the circuit. I would wait until the finish area; where the most people were, because I wanted to make a name for myself. And usually the riders were all huddled to one side of the road and I'd take the other side of the road and wait for the crowd and I'd just ride past them. And they'd start jumping to get on my wheel and they just couldn't. I could go 6 kph faster than anyone else.'

To his surprise, he didn't get a pro contract. There were no offers. Disappointing for him but fortuitous for Britain because, awkward or not, there was no way a man with that record could be left out of the team for either the world road or track championships in 1967.

The track came first, in Amsterdam, and to nobody's surprise Webb and the team manager, Dave Handley, had a barney and fell out. Nobody who knows both men's temperament was surprised. Webb had arranged to leave Amsterdam with his mentor, Charles Ruys. But when Ruys didn't show up, he fell in instead with Albert Beurick, a fat Belgian bar-owner who had befriended many Britons including Tom Simpson. Beurick took him to Destelbergen in Belgium and there Webb lapped the field twice on a four-kilometre circuit. A few days later he cycled the 300 kilometres to that part of Holland that nudges the German border and where the road championships were to be held at Heerlen.

In the crucial phase, there were four riders away – Ampler, Monsere, Conti and Benn. Webb realised almost too late that he was riding for fifth place and looked around for help in a chase. It didn't come.

There was an Italian in the four-man break and three Italians with me, and there was a Belgian away and I had De Vlaeminck, and Pijnen wasn't going to work. So the last lap, I went to the front, with the wind coming from the left, and I stayed to the right. I could have got up on my own but, I thought, when I get there I'm going to be knackered. I'm going to be fifth anyway. I started to work out how I was going to do it. I would open the sprint [away from the bunch] slowly. The best blokes would stay with me. I went to the front and I reckoned if we could get them in sight before the last climb, someone's going to try to jump over to the leaders.

And come to the last, sure enough, we got them in sight, and they were attacking as well, and the speed was going up and down, and they started coming from behind me, trying to jump on to them, which is what I wanted.

So we went up the last climb and they were attacking all the time and I stayed on the back, just leaving them to it, just being towed up, which was perfect. I'd never suffered that much in my life before. I'd just done seven kilometres in the front and I was just having to hold these blokes.

Everything came together 32 kilometres from the finish, and I decided halfway through the race that if we were together, I should go away. Everyone went right for the bend and I went to the left, flat out. It may sound bigheaded but I knew I could ride faster than everyone else. I was training 200 to 300 kilometres a day and the World Championship was only 198, so I was well within myself. I took 30 metres from that corner. I saw I had a gap and I thought if I can take the last corner without falling on my head, I was world champ.

And it was one of the easiest races I'd ever ridden. Everything I'd planned happened. I crossed the line and the first thing I thought was: 'Were there only four blokes ahead of me? Were there any more?' I put my arm in the air, but I thought: 'What have I done?'

What he had done was become World Road Champion. No Briton has done it since, three and a half decades later. He got a professional contract, with Raymond Poulidor at Mercier, but it didn't work out and his career as a pro fizzled out after two years. That doesn't take away from his World Championship, of course. His neighbours know who he is and, as a veteran, he even became a Belgian champion in one of the country's lesser classes.

He never came home from Belgium. He bought himself a house in Wachtebeke and parked his MG-B outside it. He got himself a job in the docks where, he said, he was 'the best paid crane driver in Belgium'. The idea of returning to Britain never arose.

It did, though, for the other male world champion. He was all for going back to Britain, perhaps to try to build a professional team there. But he didn't make it either. Not alive, anyway. Tom Simpson's death in the Tour has overshadowed much of what he did. And there is a sad irony that his World Road Championship in 1965, the first for a British professional, set off the events that killed him. Denied by his broken leg a chance to cash in on his rainbow jersey, he set out to get a yellow one instead. That was how he died, trying to make it happen.

The 1965 World Championship, held in continuous rain at Lasarte, near San Sebastian in northern Spain, had the same advantage as the 1967 Tour. Freed from his obligation to Peugeot, Simpson could ride for Britain, knowing that few of his British team-mates could help him but, equally, that few were in a position to hinder. If things went right, he could take his chance; if they went wrong, he could sell his services to someone else.

Things went right. The race was 14 laps of 19 kilometres, a race of six and a half hours. Simpson attacked two laps from the finish on the big climb near Hernani. He kept his bike in 53 x 14 and only the German, Rudi Altig, stayed with him. Altig speaks no English, so Simpson shouted to him in French.

'Come on Rudi,' he said. 'Remember the Baracchi!' That was a reference to the two-man time-trial held in Italy at the end of each season and at that time hugely popular. Simpson and Altig had been partners the previous year and the German had shattered Simpson in the same way he had shattered Jacques Anquetil in 1962. Altig had ended up literally pushing Anquetil and he all but had to do the same to Simpson.

'I must have made him think he could win,' Simpson said. 'He just smiled and nodded and we got down to the work of keeping clear. I started my sprint a few hundred yards out and kept going as hard as I could. And I was over the line, grinning like a maniac, heart pounding and tears welling up in my eyes.'

The improbability that the weedy, if courageous, Simpson could even get to the line with Altig, let alone outsprint him, provoked shouts of 'Fix!'

The cycling wholesaler Ron Kitching, who was there, said: 'I remember asking Tom about when he and Altig were together in the lead. I asked him what they said to each other. Tom had that deadpan expression on his face and I probed. "You must have said something, alone together in the lead of the world championship." Tom told me that Altig spoke first and asked how much he would take in payment to lose the race. Tom said, "I then asked him how much he would take to lose. End of conversation." And I am convinced that he told me the truth.'

And that's been the belief ever since. Unlikely though it was, Simpson the non-sprinter beat Altig the charging bull. Nobody has ever said otherwise. And yet had the race been just half an hour longer it would never have happened. Simpson's white Peugeot was grabbed and disappeared as crowds milled around him. Conscious of the need to placate his sponsor, he pulled a white team jersey over the blue and red of his British colours and went to the rostrum in that instead, for which he was fined.

When he finally got the bike back, it was to find a two-inch strip ripped from the rear tread, with strands of rubber hanging free. It was bulging at the side and on the point of bursting. If there is no doubt about the honesty of the win, there are considerable doubts about just who took Simpson's dope test for him. Those who were there name a name, and it wasn't Simpson's. That was both typical of the era and of cycling in general and it would have sad echoes when Simpson died in a drugged state two years later, trying to make amends for the bad luck the rainbow jersey had brought him. Simpson died in July 1967. The cause was well known.

Sadly, some weren't paying attention. A domestic professional and part-time cabinetmaker from Buckinghamshire, Roger Newton, came second in that year's British professional championship with the help of amphetamine. He blamed a vitamin pill bought in Switzerland. He was followed by Albert Hitchen in the Tour of the West, also drugged with amphetamine, and by the Londoner, Martin Filmer, who refused to take a test.

Then came the world championships in Holland, the ones in which Webb won his amateur championship and Beryl Burton – of whom much more later – won the last of hers. The romantic saw their wins as a tribute to Simpson, but his death had had a more practical bearing. The UCI was forced to take drug-taking more seriously. Its secretary, René Chésal, said: 'This will be the first guaranteed dope-free world cycling championships, of that we can be sure.' Which could only have meant that those before 1967 *hadn't* been dope-free. Including 1965, presumably. Of 1967, he could have meant either that riders had learned their lesson or that those who hadn't would be flung out. It soon became obvious that the second was the more obvious. By the first Saturday evening, Yvonne Reynders and Alex Boeye of Belgium, Dieter Kemper of Germany, Freddy Ruegg of Switzerland and Kevin Crowe of Australia had all been disqualified as drug-takers.

All of which makes Britain's two world champions on the road all the more meretricious. But why aren't there more? A question to ponder for a while.

18

A SCANDAL ON WHEELS

It was no surprise that Miss America was chased and jeered during Paris–Rouen back in the nineteenth century. Some of the shouting was good-natured, of course, but the idea of women riding bikes, let along racing them, had been a scandal since cycling began.

Dick Swann, a British enthusiast who worked for years as a preacher in America – he died in 2003 – put the first race for women as a two-mile track event in Ashfield, in New South Wales, Australia, in 1888. If he's right, that makes the first female winner a Miss Dot Morrell.

The structure of women's racing was even looser than the men's. The routine for both was that promoters ran races as stunts, either to sell newspapers or, originally, to bring spectators past the ticket office. The historian Jim McGurn says: 'The mixing of athleticism and femininity [women raced in skirts which showed their thighs] seems to have been a major voyeuristic attraction to male customers, and a boon to profits.' For that reason, he suspects, *vélocipèdeuses* may not have been simply spirited daughters of the aristocracy, but hired actresses.

For the serious, there were unregistered world championships all over the place. And, since women raced for money, or at least for expensive trophies that could be sold, many were effectively professionals. They rode tracks alone and behind pacers and they established road records.

Clara Grace took the national track championship in 1895, the road championship in 1896, and the London–Brighton–London (7:14:0), Coventry–London (6:3:17) and 50-mile records. In 1895 she took on the 'unbeatable' Lisette, nickname of the French woman Amélie le Gall (who, incidentally, was trained and managed by Choppy Warburton). Lisette rode for Gladiator, the company that supplied one of the pacing teams at the Catford Chain Race, and won the first official World Championship in 1896. Other Gladiator riders won in 1897 and 1899 (Hélène Dutrieu) and in 1898 (Louise Roger, also one of Warburton's riders).

Grace took on Lisette in a 40-kilometre challenge race at the Parc des Princes – and demolished her reputation as 'unbeatable'. On 29 November 1895 she beat her again in an 80-kilometre race on the Westminster track in London.

Times changed after that and, just as cycling turned against racing on the roads, so it also turned against women racing anywhere. The *American Cycling Gazette* said in November 1898: 'Female racing is to be deplored for reasons which have on many occasions been tersely and forcibly stated; but while the public popularise these exhibitions, so will enterprising promoters shame the racing path by holding them.'

Cycling refused to print the results of women's races and, one by one, the foreign stars disappeared: Louise Roger became a car-racer; Lisette married a rancher in Argentina; Hélène Dutrieu became a stunt rider, looping the loop at circuses on barrel-shaped tracks.

In Britain the situation was splendidly illustrated by the episode of the Hautboy Hotel in Ockham in Surrey. The date was 27 October 1898. It was on that morning that an aristocrat called Florence Wallace Harberton set off from her home in Cromwell Road in the posh London district of Kensington to have lunch in the countryside.

Everything about her suggests that she knew the outrage that her outfit would cause, although these days it's hard to see what the fuss was about. She was wearing not shorts and a tight jersey but a jacket and a pair of exceptionally long and baggy knickerbockers, trousers which gathered just above the ankle and showed a short length of sock. It was called Rational Dress, because progressives considered it more rational, or logical, than the full-length dresses that women were expected to wear. Viscountess Harberton knew the fuss she would cause and provoked it whenever she could; indeed, she was president of the Western Rational Dress Society.

The chances are that she chose the Hautboy Hotel deliberately. It was run by Mrs Marta Sprague, a fearsome-sounding woman who had objected to women riding the nearby Ripley Road – now the A3 – in tights. If Florence Harberton wanted a fight, she would find it at the Hautboy.

The hotel – pronounced *hoe-boy* – had been built in neo-Gothic style 33 years earlier by the Earl of Lovelace, Lord Lieutenant and therefore the Queen's representative to Surrey. It's still there and so are the five coats of arms in the prize-winning brickwork, each topped by the Earl's coronet.

Florence, an aristocrat herself, propped up her bike and asked to be served. Mrs Sprague took one look and showed her into the bar parlour. The editor of the CTC's *Gazette*, E. R. Shipton, said: 'The room ... was already tenanted by three men who were smoking and drinking. As a consequence, the complainant [Florence Harberton] was practically compelled to leave the house and ride some three miles further to get the refreshment of which she stood in need.' The point being that in those days to show any lady, let alone a toff, into a room of working men was a great insult and worse than simply showing her the door. It wasn't much better than accusing her of prostitution.

As it happened, Florence was a member of the Cyclists' Touring Club and the Hautboy was one of its registered hotels. The CTC complained, Mrs Sprague said she didn't care and that she'd do it again, and so the CTC went to court to complain that its contract with the hotel had been broken. In fact, the CTC lost when the case went to its second stage and the hotel produced fanciful pictures of the workmen's bar that showed it as a five-star paradise. But it had been a brave move on behalf of a brave, if doubtless difficult, woman because at that time most CTC members, and certainly its hierarchy, were firmly against Rational Dress. Freddie Bidlake ridiculed it as Laughable Dress and insisted that the CTC was defending not the right to wear knickerbockers but the principle of a contract that all cyclists would be served.

Of the way women ought to behave, he wrote: 'A skirtless lady on tour is bound to suffer much. She is singularly conspicuous, a centre of observation and exposed to such contumelious ridicule as the ordinary sensitive feminine nature hesitates to provoke.' And of their actually racing, he vapoured: 'Cycle racing for women is generally acknowledged to be undesirable. The stylish, clever lady stops short of being a scorcher, but if women's races were to be organised, the participants would have to run their limit, or else make a mockery of racing. And that limit is not pleasant to contemplate ... the speed woman, dishevelled, grimy and graceless.'

He would have hated Tessie Reynolds. She was just 16 and being dishevelled and grimy and working up a muck sweat was just what she liked best. Where Hélène Dutrieu and her colleagues were fêted in France, Reynolds was ridiculed in 1893 for riding the 110 miles from London to Brighton and back in eight and a half hours. *Cycling* said her ride caused 'real pain, not unmixed with disgust'. What's more, she had worn trousers and been paced by men, which had spread the outrage out into the non-cycling public as well.

Not wishing to cause further illness to the nation, she compromised for photographs after the ride by sitting on a woman's bike without a top tube – she had raced on a 'man's' bike – and wore a hat and flouncy blouse.

Women's racing, pretty much squashed by the attitudes of society in general and of cycling with it, would have progressed faster had the rest of the sport progressed faster. But officials saw things differently then, and worried about things that no longer concern us. The battle between the NCU, the RTTC and the BLRC seemed far more important than securing the sport's future by opening it up to the other half of the population.

They did still race, of course. It was just that they weren't taken seriously. The BLRC had a small programme but, says Eileen Gray, later the leading light in organised women's racing, there was nothing on closed circuits under NCU rules until external events forced one. 'It was only when we received an invitation to a three-day in France that the Whitewebbs CC [in north London] put on an event at an airfield so we could select a team,' she said. 'In spite of the lack of experience, those first six girls did very well and Millie Robinson won the event in Roanne in 1955.'

Gray's assessment is that Roanne persuaded the UCI that the support was there for women's racing. It certainly had its effect in Britain because the Women's Cycle Racing Association began the following season, in May 1956, to give Britain its first national road championship. The WCRA had grown from a similar organisation started for track riders in 1949.

Riders taking part were known, as they would continue to be known well into the era of equal opportunities that affected the rest of the world, as 'ladies'. It is a title that Bernard Thompson uses throughout his history of time-trialling, *Alpaca to Skin Suit*, published as late as 1988. Thompson is a gentle man who has done more for the sport than many realise and his choice of word probably reflects his era rather than anything deeper. But it's illustrative of the way cycling saw itself not as a sport for all, but as a sport for men in which women were allowed under set circumstances.

Women were 'ladies' while the men were never 'gentlemen'. Men's races were simply races; women's races were 'ladies' events'. It was as though the rule book insisted that 'unless otherwise stated, the word "race" shall mean "men's race"'.

The WCRA faced a battle. Thompson says of the approaching end of wartime Britain: 'Although male time-triallists now had a full programme of national championships and a season-long BAR competition to keep motivation simmering steadily throughout 1944, the women had just one target, a national 25-mile championship.' The '50' didn't come until 1948 (won by Stella Farrell in 2:21:31), the '100' until 1950 (Eileen Sheridan 4:37:53).

The opposition the WCRA faced went well east of Dover. International cycling fought hard against including women in world championships. The first were in Reims in France in 1958, says Eileen Gray. 'We went to Liège in Belgium in 1959, after which the UCI stated that they would allow them to be split from the men in future.' That was a blessing to the Dutch, who were happy to hold the men's championships in 1959 but, says Gray, 'so disagreed with women racing that we were not included in the programme. The Belgians put our events on in Liège'. Not that things went altogether well on the equal opportunities front even there. 'It was in Liège that I was thrown out of the official banquet in spite of having an invite and that I was a delegate and team manager – because I was a woman.' Of that, though, more later.

For the moment, let's return to that name Eileen Sheridan, the winner of the first 100-mile championship. Ron Kitching said of her: 'She was a wonderful kid. I don't think anyone could fault her for anything. She was and is always charming, polite. How she performed so well as an athlete with such a nice personality is beyond me. There was no nastiness, no aggression. She didn't seem to want to beat anyone. She just used to like to cycle and I think it was really just as easy as that for Eileen.'

Eileen Sheridan won the BBAR in 1949 and then again in 1950, after which *Cycling* observed that: 'It may well be that Eileen Sheridan will go down in cycling history as the greatest of all riders.' She broke records at 30, 50, 100 miles and 12 hours and won all three national championships. As with Ken Joy and other long-distance time-triallists, though, she had nowhere else to go. Joy could at least have turned to circuit and road-racing, but that wasn't a choice open to Sheridan. Instead, like Joy, she turned professional for Hercules.

She took all 20 women's records, including the 24-hour with 446.25 miles and Land's End–John o'Groats, in 1954 when she was 32, in 2:11:7. Like Dick Poole years later, she too continued for the 1,000 miles. Her manager, Frank Southall, asked her if she could ride a third of a mile an hour faster. When Sheridan asked him why, he told her it was because she could beat the men's record if she did. Sheridan recalled:

When I replied that I didn't think I could, he told me: 'In that case you're going to stop and take a proper rest.' When I told him I had been hallucinating, Frank responded, 'Don't worry, we're all seeing things that aren't there. We could all do with some sleep'.

We had a caravan mounted on the back of an articulated lorry, which wasn't such a good idea as it was rather difficult to climb up into it, especially when the legs were a bit wobbly. I remember really craving for salt. They rustled me up two eggs and four rashers of bacon, which hardly sounds like racing food but it was just the job.

Still interested in the sport and living beside the Thames, she carved the cut-glass goblet given to Chris Boardman at the RTTC dinner after he won his Olympic medal.

Cycling's assessment of her as the greatest female rider was valid at the time and is still sustainable now. She reached the top in everything open to her. No other rider has held all the national records at one go, and the fact that she was denied both road-racing and a chance at world championships can hardly be held against her.

Eileen Sheridan taking a drink from Frank Southall at Hyde Park during the London–Oxford–London record, June 1952

As Eileen Gray pointed out, the resistance to women racing internationally was so great that in 1959 the Dutch, a nation usually associated with tolerance and progressive ideas, just refused to allow them into their world championships. Britain sent a team to Liège instead, telling each rider to get to London, where they'd be given £2 to find somewhere to stay and eat. From there they were to go on to Belgium as cheaply as they could.

Beryl Burton, selected only as a reserve, travelled at the last minute. She went to Dover, took the ferry to Ostend, then crossed

Belgium in the car of a friend, Tom Feargrove. It was 'a converted banger called Britannia,' Eileen Gray recalled. 'Tom and his old American semi-bus was a legend, and he is still remembered for his efforts for all the girls and still comes to the WCRA annual lunch. He used to pick up riders all the way down the North Road from Yorkshire.'

Feargrove's son, Ernie, became the women's international mechanic.

Feargrove senior's first pickup on many trips south was Beryl Burton. She is the only rider with a record comparable to Sheridan's. Exact comparisons are impossible and it may be that Burton would have come out on top had the two raced in the same era. As it is, it's impossible to say, and in 1958 nobody would have tried. Burton was lucky to be at the championships, not only because she'd been told to wait at home until someone dropped out, but because she knew little about the 3,000-metre pursuit she was to ride.

She walked around the centre of the big rough track at Liège in plain trousers and a gabardine jacket, because there were no tracksuits. Her wheels were shabby and her husband, Charlie, had found her shellac to stick on the tyres only just before she left. Millie Robinson, another British rider (Manx, more strictly, but riding for Britain), lent her a better set. On them, Burton won the championship by 0.1 second from Elsy Jacobs of Luxembourg. She then waited for the road-race, where she came fifth to one of her consistent rivals, Yvonne Reynders of Belgium.

When Burton got back to Leeds as Britain's first female World Champion, it was to find nobody at the station. Charlie was at home with their young daughter, Denise. The new champion muttered a bit, then set off to walk to the suburb of Morley, where she lived. It was a struggle, with two bikes and a big bag. A lorry driver took pity and drove her home.

Travel to the 1960 championships was hardly any more glamorous. They were in Leipzig, in what was then East Germany. Burton travelled late so she could ride the national '100' championship. The delay was worth her while because she won by 11:19 and reduced the record to 4:18:19, but it exacted its cost hours later.

She flew to Berlin after the ride and arranged to meet Charlie from the train from Leipzig. He arrived late, though, because of a hold-up and they both missed their train back as a result.

She said: 'There we were, stuck in East Berlin. The police [who recognised her] asked us what we were doing, and we explained and then they put us in a hotel. We hadn't a bean between us and they offered us breakfast. We refused, not knowing how we were going to pay for it. We didn't know we didn't have to pay for it, and we were absolutely starving. There were soldiers on the train with bayonets and Charlie said, "Let's forget the world's!"'

It was as well they didn't: she won both the pursuit and the road-race. 'I put my head down and imagined I was riding a 25-mile time-trial,' she said in *Personal Best* of how she rode away from Elsy Jacobs.

By the end of her career, she had won seven world championships, 74 national championships, 50 competition records and 25 consecutive BBARs. There has always been much less competition among women than between the more numerous men, but even so, her 100-plus championships are four times greater than the 25 of Ian Hallam between 1969 and 1982, which fell within Burton's career. In fact she'd have won the men's BBAR in 1974 if she'd done all her best rides in that year.

Something of the sort seemed possible in 1967 when she was first starter in the Otley 12-hour in Yorkshire. Normally the best riders are placed at the end of the field, but putting Burton first meant she was only two minutes behind the fastest in the men's event just before hers. In those days men and women weren't allowed to compete together, even in time-trialling, so the extra minute between Mike McNamara, best of the men, and Beryl Burton, best of the women was the ludicrous, but legal, way of confirming that these were two races and that McNamara and Burton weren't competing against each other.

It was nonsense, of course, but then so was the original rule. Far from being two races, there was nothing but incentive for Burton and nothing but disadvantage for McNamara. He would gain nothing if he beat Burton, because he was a man against a woman. But Burton would be a heroine for beating McNamara, and have nothing but sympathy if she didn't. She was, after all, a woman. When Burton said at the start that she was 'just out for a day's ride to enjoy myself', the pressure on McNamara was even greater. He risked going flat out, but still being caught by a woman 'enjoying herself'.

After 156 miles there were still the original two minutes between them. By 180 miles McNamara had stretched them out to nine. By 235 miles both were on the circuit of roads they would each follow until their time ran out. And there, finally, Burton passed him.

'Would you like a liquorice allsort?' she asked, reducing cycling history to the mundane.

'Ta, love,' McNamara said and Burton, having fulfilled the offer, cruised by. The challenge had pushed him to 276.52 miles, almost five better than Owen Blower's record of nine years earlier. He won the BBAR. Burton, on the other hand, finished at 277.25 miles and pushed the women's record beyond the men's for the first time. Not at all the sort of woman that Bidlake would have liked.

The cycling cartoonist Johnny Helms, by the way, always considered it a shame that McNamara ate the allsort. His view was that it should have been put on display in a darkened room where the unworthy could pay homage.

Beryl Burton won the World Road Championship twice, winning alone, won the World Pursuit title five times and the BBAR from 1959 to 1983. Her 12-hour in 1967 remained the country's best for two years until John Watson rode 281.87 in 1969. Her BBAR average of 24.491 mph in 1967 was better than all but four riders in the men's competition.

Her last World Championship was in Montreal in 1974. She got no further than the quarter-finals in the pursuit and finished fifth in the road-race. The style of road-racing had begun changing. Clare Greenwood, a later British international, said of the era that 'most of the field were like Michelin women'. Now riders were leaner and more athletic. They rode more like men, in fast bursts. It was a style that an ageing Burton couldn't handle. She had grown up in long-distance time-trialling, with the power to ride fast for protracted distances. Riders who knew they would never catch her if she got away – Burton almost always won alone – began to attack, knowing she couldn't respond. Instead of respect and fear, they treated her as they had started to treat each other.

Beryl Burton, after winning a quarter-final 3,000m pursuit at the World Championships in 1960

That is the way things still are in women's racing. Gone are the strong, square riders of the 1950s and 1960s. Instead, the women's road-race looks a junior men's race but with short riders.

Bitterness came into her racing and it showed with her daughter Denise, now grown from the little child who kept her father Charlie at home when Beryl arrived back from her first World Championship. Denise had, herself, become an international. In 1975 she won a stage race in Le Havre that her mother had won previously. Beryl did not take the message of mortality easily. It showed when she and Denise and a third rider, Carol Barton, reached the finish of the national road-race championship that same year. Barton and Burton Sr were of the old mould; Burton Jr was of the new style. And Burton Jr won.

There was no maternal delight. 'It would be nice to record that I felt pleased for her as I heard the judges' decision announced,' she told Dennis Donovan of *Cycling*. 'But this is not a story for some romantic magazine. It was a real-life narrative about basically ordinary people with jangled nerves and emotions. Our bitter conflict played out in gladiatorial fashion.'

That 'bitter conflict' included the mother's resentment, or at least feeling of injustice, that she had been beaten not only by a younger rider, but one who did nothing all day but train. Beryl worked throughout her career, most colourfully as a rhubarb-picker for her clubmate Nim Carline.

The argument split Beryl's household because Charlie didn't agree. The row went on for two years, great entertainment for those not caught in the crossfire but bitter for the protagonists. Denise, though, had years on her side. Mother and daughter rode against each other in the semi-final of the pursuit at the national championship at Leicester in 1977. The multiple World Champion was humbled from the gun as her daughter began gaining on her.

Beryl finished third, Denise took the silver and, for all it matters now except to her, Margaret Gordon-Smith won. Dennis Donovan wrote:

Watching from the press box that day, I could see Beryl wearily get off her bike, her shoulders slumped in defeat with her back to her daughter. Denise walked over to face her mother and suddenly the two women were in each other's arms, and the rift had been healed.

It would be nice to say that everyone lived happily afterwards, but life isn't like that, and when Denise's marriage broke down she became ill, suffering from the wasting disease, anorexia nervosa.

While Denise recovered and remarried, Beryl developed breast cancer and had a mastectomy. On 5 May 1996 she was found dead beside the road, having crashed going down a hill. She was 58. There is now a commemoration garden in Morley.

Ron Kitching, who had made Charlie his warehouse manager, and let Beryl help herself to whatever she wanted, said:

> The way the sport went for her must have made her a very ruthless person. Somewhere along the line there has to be a breaking point, a moment when you are prepared to let someone else win, at last. But I don't think that ever came to Beryl. She just didn't want anyone else to better her. But it must have become boring in the end. I used to try to persuade her to do something else, to go for road records like Eileen Sheridan did. But I don't think the money was there to support her.

The contrast between the old order and new showed with the arrival in 1974 of a young girl with long dark hair and a skinny frame that made both her shorts and jersey hang loose on her body. Amanda Ellen Jones had been out on club runs in Lancashire and found she could hold her own with the rest. So she entered a time-trial. A picture taken of the rider waiting to start a minute ahead of her shows her standing nervously behind, waiting to see what happened next.

What happened next, or at any rate later, was that she became World Road Champion at Goodwood, Sussex, in 1982. As her entry in the *Golden Book of Cycling* says:

> Mandy Jones is the perfect example of how a youngster, while enjoying the companionship and adventure of club runs, can successfully aspire to becoming a world champion by self-dedication and encouragement.

Five years after her first race, Jones won the junior '10' championship in a tie with another Lancashire girl, Julie Earnshaw. Their time, 25:42, persuaded Jones she'd prefer racing to club riding.

In 1980 she came third to the little American, Beth Heiden, in the world road-race at Sallanches, beneath Mont Blanc. Heiden disappeared from the sport almost immediately, but Jones stuck around.

Having won the national 3,000-metre pursuit, she broke the world 5,000-metre record at Leicester and won the national '50' championship. Then, that autumn she won the World Championship in the rolling hills of Sussex. Jones broke away and won by 10 seconds, Britain's first woman road champion of the world for 15 years.

'I won by accident,' she said. 'It was just plain daft. We were going downhill and I just rode past them. Then I looked back, saw I had a gap and kept going. I was praying my legs wouldn't collapse. But with around half a lap to go, I started thinking,"Hey, I could win this!"'

The links with Beryl Burton, the woman she succeeded, were obvious: the talent for time-trialling, the pursuit championship and the lone break. But otherwise the two were as different as Burton's curls and Jones' raven pudding-basin. Burton was steady, strong and powerful; Jones was all those but light on the pedals and nippy as well. The kind of woman who'd brought Burton's era to a close, in fact.

Since then, another has come as well. Nicole Cooke twice won the world road-race, the time-trial and the mountain bike race championship as a junior, then won six races on the Continent in 2002, her first season as a senior. To her, too, fell the women's World Cup. Of her potential as a successor to Mady Jones and Beryl Burton, *Procycling* editor Jeremy Whittle writes: 'Nicole's great strength is her determination and work ethic. Her ambition is immense and with expert advice she could be the dominant force in women's racing for a decade.'

19

UN MILLAR PEUT EN CACHER
UN AUTRE

Every bar in France has a sign warning of the consequences of public drunkenness. Similarly, every railway crossing has a warning that *un train peut en cacher un autre* – one train can hide another. In other words, watch out because two can come at the same time, and if one doesn't get you then the other one will. That's how it has been in Britain with Millars. Not just two – first Robert and then David – but both spelled with the less usual A before the R.

The death of Tom Simpson in the 1967 Tour de France left a void in British cycling. It had seemed almost too late to believe that a Briton could win the race and now, without doubt, it was. Nearly half a century on, there has still been no one from the island kingdom off the European mainland who has come remotely near. Barry Hoban won the stage from Carpentras to Sète on 14 July, the day after Simpson's death, when the Frenchman Jean Stablinski, and others, insisted that one of the hotchpotch British team ride ahead of the race all day in respectful homage.

'I just found myself at the front,' Hoban said. 'I can tell you every inch of the Ghent–Wevelgem that I won, but even to this day nothing of that stage of the Tour.' Vin Denson, logically the man to have led the stage because he was Simpson's closest friend in the team, denies Hoban's version and says not only that he, Denson, had been offered the tribute but that Hoban had ridden fast enough that the rest had had to chase. Given that Hoban says he remembers nothing of what happened and that Denson's version is unproven, the best that should happen is that the pair be left to argue it out between them.

Hoban remains bitter to this day at what he perceives as his lack of recognition in Britain. He is fêted on the continent, he says, but in Britain he is 'just someone who rode the Tour de France a few years ago; so what?' In fact, Hoban, who in March 1962 packed in a job as a colliery apprentice to try his luck in Arras in northern France, spent 18 years abroad, rode 12 Tours, finished 11, and won eight stages. The first was the Simpson memorial stage, the last at Bordeaux in 1975.

André Bertin, a cycle dealer, gambler and whisky importer who gave Hoban a contract as an independent in the Bertin–Porter 39 team, wanted to build a professional team around him. Hoban's decision to sign for Raymond Poulidor's Mercier–BP team in 1964 made more sense in that it was the bigger and surer team but it angered Bertin, who called him an idiot and predicted that 'he'll end up as nothing but a domestique to Poulidor', which turned out to be true.

Poulidor's greatest talent lay in the mountains, though, where he wasn't a star but could match all but the best. He needed fast riders to keep him in contention on the flatter stages, and Hoban was among the fastest. Since Poulidor couldn't sprint and Hoban could, the arrangement gave the Yorkshireman *carte blanche* in the gallops. The result was that Hoban had the novelty of winning little outside the Tour but being a contender for one-off honours within it. The position is usually the opposite.

Lack of success outside the Tour, though, meant he was no claimant to Simpson's title. He was a lightning finisher, but had nothing of Simpson's slogging power and often dangerous bravery. With both men off the scene, Britain lacked both a slogger and a sprinter. It had nobody but a few brave souls who did their best, raised hopes, rode to the limit of their talents, and then vanished. And then came Robert Millar.

Millar – Bob to fellow professionals – came second in the Vuelta in 1985 and 1986 (the first ride making him Scotland's sports personality of the year), second in the Giro in 1987, and fourth in the Tour in 1984. No Briton has finished the Tour better or come closer to winning one of the three main Tours. His tenacity and wiriness made him one of the best climbers of the era, and he won the mountains competition of the Tour de France in 1984. But just as many gifted climbers pay for their closeness to the angels by the hell of their looks, so Millar was said by the writer Robin Magowan that 'with his distinctive pointy nose he looks more like a Dickensian chimney-sweep'. A French writer said his tiny stature reminded him of an *asticot*, or maggot, and the nickname stuck.

Millar moved to the ACBB club in Paris after winning the British Amateur Championship in 1978 when he was 20. He won thirteen races in his first year to become the best amateur in France. He came fourth in the World Amateur Championship in 1979 after pulling his foot out in the sprint. That brought him a contract as a pro with Peugeot.

Millar was never the easiest man to get close to, though, and he barely got on with Peugeot's manager, Maurice De Muer. That meant he didn't ride the Tour until Roland Berland took over the team in 1983. Then he broke away on the Pyresourde, won by six seconds and moved up 56 places to 27th as well as coming second in the mountains competition. By stage 13 he became the first Briton to wear the polka-dot jersey. Next year he won in the mountains outright and finished fourth overall.

In 1985 it all started going wrong after starting so well. To this day nobody knows why he didn't win the Vuelta. He led for nine days, until the last but one stage. It was then that Pedro Delgado and another Spaniard, Jose Recio, got seven minutes' lead in 60 kilometres and won by 6:50.

Millar reckoned he would have been helped had he had more friends in the sport. He blamed Berland for not giving him better time checks. Berland said he hadn't had them from the organisers. The organisers denied it, and said they'd given them every three minutes. There were then claims that Spanish riders had ganged up against him, even that the conservative Spanish didn't want their national tour won by a long-haired vegetarian with an earring.

Millar's team-mates claimed they hadn't helped because a railway crossing had delayed them for several minutes, 'only the train never came'. Some people said the French Peugeot team didn't want their foreigner to win a big tour. Pick the reason or reasons that suit you best.

In 1995 Millar joined the doomed Le Groupement team, which ran out of money and folded in mid-1995, ending his career. His last big race was that year's Manx International, which was also the national championship. He won alone.

Millar remains a contradiction to this day. He is determinedly Scottish yet he moved to Daventry in the English midlands and rarely speaks well of Glasgow. He is taciturn and even abusive. Of reporters in the Tour he once said: 'Guys see the race on TV, then ask you what's happened. You see them sleeping during the day because they've been drunk the night before. If I think they're useless, I tell them so.' His career as national coach was short-lived. Perhaps as a result.

Millar remains Britain's best roadman since Simpson and the best Tour de France rider the country has ever had. Sean Yates won the time-trial of the 1988 Tour at Wasquehal; Malcolm Elliott won two stages of the Vuelta in 1989; and then Yates took the Tour's yellow jersey for a while in 1994, and Chris Boardman wore it that year and in 1998. And yet, every rider since the 1960s has lived in Simpson's shadow as Britain repeatedly tries to claim a place in a foreign sport. In the 1970s *Cycling* was reduced to cheering for Dutchmen simply because they rode British bikes made in Raleigh's factory at Nottingham. Since then the flag has been waved for anyone who simply speaks English, be they Irish, American, Australian or South African. It's hard to imagine that the Dutch thought of the Raleigh team as anything but Dutch, or that Americans even notice, let alone feel any allegiance with, some game but struggling Brit at the back of the bunch.

The pressure on Chris Boardman to be the next big thing was stifling. In the hope of British fans Boardman was promoted from a brilliant, if unstable, prologue rider into a potential Tour winner. It was a hope polished further when he was named as leader of his team, Crédit Agricole. Boardman deserves no criticism for the way he rode because he consistently gave his best. But he was leader of his team only in the sense that generals lead their armies from the rear.

Riding round France once during the Tour, a man in a bar near Limoges spotted my accent and asked what prospects I saw for my fellow countrymen. I said I didn't really see any prospects at all, that usually being the case, but that I would look out for them nevertheless.

'And Monsieur Chris?' he said, using the name that the TV commentators had taken to using and pronouncing it *Chreees*.

'He's not riding this year,' I said.

'Ah non?'

'No, he pulled out with a few days to go.'

My new friend shrugged in the French way. 'Ah well,' he said, 'it'll save him doing it later.'

That was the French view of Boardman. He was popular in France, well liked and admired, but – on the road – he was seen as never more than a time-trial specialist. He rode the Tour's fastest prologue at his first attempt in 1994, riding at 55.152 kph in Lille to beat Miguel Indurain by 15 seconds. His yellow jersey was Britain's first since Simpson's, 32 years earlier. The French don't mind time-trial specialists. The ultimate, after all, was Jacques Anquetil. But the difference was that Anquetil stayed upright, come what may – Boardman's minute and a half before crashing out of the prologue in St-Brieuc in 1995 is the shortest ever participation in a Tour de France – and he got through the mountains and won five Tours.

Boardman – we'll come back to him in more detail later – was a great rider in the mould of British specialists at short, fast distances, riders like Hugh Porter, Sean Yates, Barry Hoban and Norman Sheil. And then came another, David Millar, also grown from the British world of time-trialling. The French took to him instantly because of his fluent French and his *accent à la Jane Birkin*. Birkin is a British actress now better known in France, where she lives. She and the Parisian Serge Gainsbourg recorded the sexually charged *Je t'aime... moi non plus* in the 1960s. Its orgasmic moaning was banned by the BBC and promptly rose to number one. The song reappears every decade or so.

When the French TV commentator Jean-Paul Ollivier asked Millar how he had such power to win a 15-kilometre prologue in his first Tour, he said: 'We have them all the time in Britain.'

Ollivier looked surprised.

'Mais si,' Millar insisted. *'Nous les appelons les 10-mile time-trials.'*

From there he was – like Boardman – built up beyond his importance, a habit that annoyed American readers of British magazines who couldn't see what the fuss was about.

The writer Philippe Le Gars said: 'To explain him, you have to look at his Anglo-Saxon spirit, his relaxed style, his lack of typical cyclist culture or even his detachment from the sport. That kind of personality isn't typical; it's far from all the clichés of the champion cyclist.'

The early hope invested in Millar inevitably couldn't match the reality. It has always been that way with riders from a country which simply can't understand why it's not better than it is and which desperately wants to be. Millar won the prologue of the Tour and he won two stages. That is pretty good. But had he won the Tour de France, he would have been pressed to win another, and then five. Such was the pressure on him and the hope that desperate British fans invested in his legs. Sadly, because of all the pressure, the whole thing fell bloodily apart.

His problem was that he took drugs, specifically the blood-booster EPO, which adds another spark plug to a cyclist's engine. EPO had been the drug of preference in cycling for a decade. For much of that time there had been no test for it. Dope-taking quickly emerged, too, to be no stranger to Millar's team, sponsored by Cofidis, a northern French money-lending agency.

Included in that team was a Frenchman called Philippe Gaumont, a man far from unknown to drug testers. On 20 January 2004, he flew back from ten days' training in Spain and looked forward to landing at Orly, Paris's second airport, and meeting his wife, Élise. She'd left their children with her parents and she and her husband planned a romantic evening in Paris 'to get to know each other all over again'. A restaurant and a hotel had been booked and a film planned. None of it happened.

Waiting along with Élise Gaumont was a small detachment from *les stups*, the French drugs squad. The police have no interest in the falsification of bike races by people taking drugs but they are intensely fascinated by the drug dealers that make that falsification possible. Rivalries and resentments exist within cycling as within all sports. Things had been said and the police had begun taking a close interest in Cofidis's Polish soigneur, known as 'Bob' because his real name was so difficult. Gaumont, a man whose history proved he knew where to get hold of drugs, was seen as worthy of questioning.

Élise Gaumont was also questioned and then released after three hours, to spend her night at the hotel alone. 'She was,' said the journalist, Christel De Taddeo, 'one of those wives likely to find EPO in the vegetable rack of their refrigerators.' Gaumont himself was questioned for longer and, seeing no reason to be the scapegoat for others, listed not only names, but a long and spectacular account of alleged drug-taking concerning members of his team. Among those he named was Millar. The two had joined Cofidis in the same year, 1997.

For a long time Millar denied the claims. He painted Gaumont as a crackpot, a man whose wish for revenge had driven him beyond reason. Gaumont himself just shrugged. He had been through it all before and now, in his mind, he was telling the truth to be shot of it all.

'Ever since I spoke out, I've been treated as an informer and a madman. That leaves me neither angry nor sad. I knew that one day I'd have to get it all off my chest. You don't drug yourself for ten years with a smile on your lips. Our lives aren't fairy tales is what I wanted to say, that's all.'

The fairy tale was about to end for Millar. Drugs police don't go for the niceties of journalists and officials. They turned over Millar's home in Biarritz, then came looking for him in a restaurant at nearby Bidart, where he was just about to start eating with a member of British Cycling's coaching team. It was 23 June.

Millar was strong on a bike, but never mentally strong off it. The police told him they'd been listening to his phone calls. They let him stew, deny what he chose, admit what he chose, then confronted him with two used syringes of Eprex (EPO) found in a hollow book at his home. Millar broke. From there he was further questioned in Nanterre by Richard Pallain, the judge leading the investigation. And his statement revealed a man torn apart by the pressures and the loneliness of bike racing, the expectations placed on him by fans back in Britain, and his inability to make close friendships, especially with women.

He spoke of how in 1999 he had despaired of cycling and began going to parties. He fell down stairs at one of them and broke a bone. It put him out of cycling for four months and he didn't get back to normal form until 2000. Winning the Tour prologue just made things worse. The contrast between the three-week 'dream' (his own word) of riding round France having been the *maillot jaune*, and the loneliness of sitting alone in his flat after it made him question his whole existence all over again. Was it worth going through all that, all the glory, all the celebrity, if all he had afterwards was a life alone in his flat with just a television set for company? Shouldn't there have been something more?

'My parents were worried,' Millar told the judge in his deposition. 'They could see that I was changing, that I was becoming more unstable. And then, that same year, at the age of 23, I fell in love. She was my first girlfriend and I felt much better about myself, that I could have a normal life, and in 2001 I raced better than ever before. I was well and strong in my head.'

Then came the Tour. His girlfriend had become his fiancée and she was there at the prologue with his parents and friends to see if he could repeat his win of the previous year. Instead, he fell off, desperately riding too fast and taking too many risks because he knew he wasn't up to winning otherwise. The rest of the race continued as miserably as it had started.

'It was during this Tour and while I was going badly, that I found myself one evening in the same bedroom as Massimilano Lelli [an ageing Italian team-mate] and he said that we were going to prepare ourselves for the Tour of Spain. He could see things were going badly between me and the team and that I wasn't even right within myself. I knew what he meant. He told me that we'd go to Italy, and I knew what that implied.'

It was in Tuscany that Millar bought his first EPO and learned how to inject it beneath the skin of his shoulder. 'I took the EPO because I knew that the Cofidis team was going to the Tour of Spain on condition that I was at the start and that I rode well. Nobody put any pressure on me but I felt it nevertheless (…) I took drugs because my job was to finish in a good place in the results. There were magazines in England, sports journalists, television stations, that wanted me to do something in the race, and I didn't want to be criticised.'

Millar was in physical and mental turmoil. 'At the start of 2002 I didn't even want to touch a bike. At the end of 2001 I went to Australia for two months with my girlfriend. Things went very badly and I ruined everything we had built together.' He came back to Europe, engaged a Spanish doctor and in May and August 2003 had two more sessions of EPO.

I put my life and my career in his hands and I gave him 12,000 euros a year. At the time, I was earning 250,000 euros in salary. That year, I won 800,000 euros. The targets we had at the end of the EPO treatment were the Dauphiné Libéré and the world time-trial championship in Canada. I had taken EPO when I was in Manchester. The two syringes found at my house were the ones with which I injected myself while I was there. I kept them to remind me that I had become World Champion at Hamilton while I was doped. I had dreamed of being World Champion but I had done it by trickery.

The UCI thought so, too. An admission of drug-taking is the same as a positive test and Millar was stripped of his title. Cofidis, which had already cleared out much of its management and, incidentally, been shown through a little-read psychiatry report to have been long troubled by drug-taking, fired him. British Cycling, with whose representative he had been when *les stups* arrived, suspended him for two years. In the time it took to read a restaurant menu, his life had crumbled into poisoned dust.

One of the last Press appointments Millar kept before the truth shattered round his ears was to pose with his immediate predecessor in the Tour, Chris Boardman, and recount the background of British international cycling. The two couldn't be more different – Millar 'like a startled chicken', in the unforgettable words of a journalist from *Procycling*, and Boardman calm and almost mathematically scholarly.

For whatever Boardman didn't manage on the road he more than made up for against the clock and on the track in particular. Cycling reporters rarely make too much of riders with early promise. So much of what promising youngsters do is a tribute to their early maturity rather than outstanding talent. History swells with riders who vanished when they moved from junior to senior or from amateur to professional, their talent having refused to move with them. For that reason nobody expected much when Boardman won the British 10-mile championship for boys in 1984.

The GHS '10', named after George Herbert Stancer, the old official, had been designed to help cycling become a sport for schools. It was open to anyone of the right age, club member or not, any sort of bike was allowed provided the gears weren't too large, and competitors would ride in the name of their school. In practice the idea failed in almost every respect because there were enough good young riders already in clubs to fill the race. Any chance visitor from outside the sport didn't stand a chance. And events were held not round town streets, where the schools were to be found, but on established time-trial courses miles away in the countryside.

*A young Chris Boardman climbing the 'Devil's Gallop'
on his way to winning the Circuit of Windermere*

The GHS '10' quickly became just another national championship and sometimes its winner went on to better things and sometimes not, in the nature of these things. Boardman went on to something better. He came to notice outside the sport when he won the Olympic 4,000-metre pursuit in Barcelona in 1992, first because his gold was Britain's first in Olympic cycling since Harry Ryan and Thomas Lance won the tandem sprint in 1920, and second because he rode a plastic bike with one front fork. It also had two sets of handlebars, one extending not sideways but forwards and the others fitted sideways to the front fork. The frame was not of tubing but a plastic monocoque made by the Lotus sports car company in Norfolk. It became known as the Superbike and secured its place in even the *Daily Star*.

Boardman had small Olympic rings tattooed behind his right shoulder. 'I wanted to immortalise my title,' he said.

The career as a professional roadman followed that, but Boardman was never at ease in bunches, rarely happy in the hills and never settled in France. He was superb in short time-trials, though, and above all in the hour record on the track.

To ride as far as possible in 60 minutes is an easily understood target and therefore one of the oldest and most prestigious in cycling. The first record is attributed to Henri Desgrange, the founder of the Tour de France, who rode 35.325 kilometres at the Buffalo track in Paris in May 1893. But that, on a track named after the Wild West shows held in the area, was just the first ratified record. There had been others before it, including some set by Britons, but not until Desgrange were the conditions internationally agreed.

The record caught on and it was broken ten times before the First World War, at which point it stood at 44.247 kilometres to Oscar Egg of Switzerland. There was a further flurry during the 1930s, then again in the 1950s, when the favoured track was the Vigorelli in Italy. Then the Dane, Ole Ritter, had the idea of exploiting the thin air of Mexico City and on 10 October, 1968, he added half a kilometre to Ferdi Bracke's record to finish in 48.653. That brought the target of 50 kilometres nearer and Eddy Merckx fell just one side on 25 October 1972, with 49.431 and Francesco Moser just the other on 19 January 1984, with 50.808 kilometres.

The Italian's record is significant in three ways. First, he beat Merckx, of whom it was said rather fancifully (he always denied it) that it had taken five years off his career. The second is that far from shortening Moser's own race prospects, he broke the record again four days later and reeled in 51.151. That nailed the reputation of the hour record as a killer of men. And third, Moser brought in the era of so-called 'funny' bikes. His had wheels of different sizes – 620mm in front and 693mm behind – and a frame of Kevlar and carbon fibre.

Merckx had ridden a conventional bike with steel tubing and spoked wheels, little more than a stripped-down road bike in appearance. Moser, on the other hand, had used spokeless, plain-sided wheels and an unusually shaped frame for maximum streamlining. The result, like the change from old-fashioned to modern springy vaulting poles, was an exceptional improvement in the record. Between 1984 and 1996, just 12 years, it improved from 50.808 to 56.375 kilometres. That's as much as the record moved between Oscar Egg in 1913 and Merckx in 1972.

The obvious reason is rarely the only one, of course, and many smaller factors also applied, like better fitness, greater incentive and smoother tracks. And, as ever, the spirit of competition. The fun of Moser's highly technical record was that it was beaten on 17 July 1993, not only on a 250m track at Hamar, north of Oslo in unfashionable Norway but by an unknown Scot, widely reported to have built his bike from washing machine parts.

Graeme Obree, who began his career as an unknown and was still pretty much a mystery until he retired, rode with his handlebars tucked under his chest. They were made in a flat-bottomed U, with the broad section held from his chest only by his hands. His arms, instead of being in any normal position, were tucked up beside him like a skier's. It was a position ridiculed by everyone who saw it and there was no surprise when he failed to beat Moser, other than that he had had the nerve to come anywhere close to it. Obree went back to his room, had a sleepless night, decided to give it another go … and rode 51.596 kilometres.

It would be surprising if there weren't some rivalry between Boardman, the Olympic champion and conventional star, and Obree, the man who had indeed fashioned bearings of his bike from an old washing machine and made a frame that had no top tube. It took six days for Boardman to better the record, using the new track at Bordeaux. The distance: 52.270 kilometres.

The record went back to Obree, now also using Bordeaux, in April 1994, when he rode 52.713. But then came bigger guns in the shape of Miguel Induráin who knocked the Scotsman permanently out of the picture at the end of the same season with 53.040.

By then the UCI had taken fright at the shape that bikes were taking and the effect they were having on records. It banned Obree's tucked-in position, a decision he snubbed by going to its exact opposite, an exceptionally stretched position immediately dubbed the Superman. His achievement was to show that an unknown rider can take on Merckx and Moser and history's other greats and that imagination can change the shape of bikes. While the crouch may have been banned, the Superman remained the standard.

Obree took refuge in the world pursuit championship whenever he was denied the hour record. When Boardman first took it, for instance, Obree won the pursuit in record time and pushed his challenger to third place. But he was never a settled man. The one attempt to forge him into a Continental team ended as pitifully as the team itself. He didn't turn up for the first day of Le Groupement's training camp and was promptly sacked.

The manager, Patrick Valcke, said: 'If a rider has that attitude, it's best to stop working together as soon as possible.' Obree had signed for the team the previous September but had missed the first get-together, in December in Florida, because he was racing on the track. Then he went to America on a personal holiday that meant he missed the team's publicity photo session. He made the next team meeting but flew to Paris instead of Lille, where the appointment was, and asked to be collected from there.

It was Robert Millar, by then a team-mate, who collected him and lectured him on the responsibilities of professionalism, of having to keep unpopular appointments. It was when they got to Lille that Valcke gave him his next unpopular appointment, along with the ticket from Glasgow to Geneva to get there. This time Valcke went to the airport himself and decided he'd had enough when his talented but troublesome Scot neither turned up nor, he said, phoned to say why.

Obree said later that he had been too ill to go, although he wouldn't say with what. The irony is that months later, just after Millar had won the British national championship, Le Groupement itself ran out of money and collapsed.

As did Obree's life. His brother Gordon died in a car crash in Scotland in October 1994 and Obree never quite got over it. He span into depression a few years later and in December 2001 a farmer's daughter found him hanging from a beam in a barn at Kilmaurs, Ayrshire. Obree, by then 36 and a father of two, had tried to kill himself. Christmas, said his wife Anne, was when Obree most missed his brother.

Meanwhile the UCI had finally had enough of the trend that Moser had started and Obree had accentuated, of bikes looking less and less like bikes and records falling, the UCI said, more through technological excess than increasing fitness. The fathers of the sport have always been concerned lest bikes become so rarefied that they price themselves out of the reach of beginners, and the UCI threw up its arms in alarm at what it considered expensive and excessive engineering on one hand and so-called improvements on the other that were no more than marketing gimmicks.

The result on the road was a severe restriction on sloping top tubes and other fads of the turn of the century and, still more dramatic, a virtual scrapping of the hour record. Both moves were bitterly criticised by those who saw bikes taking no more than their normal technological progress, but, to the UCI, the last 'genuine' hour record had been Merckx's. That was called, in English anyway, the 'sportsman's record'. There were, therefore, two records: Merckx's and Boardman's 56.375 kilometres, set in Manchester in 1996. The idea that he could no longer be formally compared to Merckx, considered by many the greatest rider ever, was too much to stand. In October 2000, just before he retired, Boardman returned to Manchester to beat Merckx's record by ten metres.

20

THIS SCEPTRED ISLE

The British track team has come a long way since the 1960s. Then, according to Graham Webb – a talented trackie as well as being world amateur road champion in 1967 – the peak of success seemed to be to demoralise the rest of the team as much as possible.

But before long the track team and the whole development of cycling came under the control of Norman Sheil, winner of the world amateur pursuit in 1955 and 1958 and a Tour de France rider for 11 stages of 1960. 'Things were in disarray when I took over as national coach,' he said after retiring and moving to Canada. 'It was the same riders they had for years who were being selected. We still had great bike riders but they were not directed or motivated enough.'

The motivation of British riders, who so often feel themselves inferior to continental opposition or at least at a disadvantage, had always been a problem. Alan Gayfer, when he was editor of *Cycling*, complained frequently that too many riders had given up hopes of winning anything long before they left Britain:

They'd persuaded themselves that the opposition was better, and so the target was simply to get into the national team. That to them was the most they could hope and it became akin to getting a medal for them. They tried hard when they were at the world championships and other events, but many clearly considered themselves on some sort of racing holiday compared to the attitude of the French and Dutch and so on, who were there to win if they could, and die if they couldn't.

With Sheil at the helm things started looking up.

I took over the national team in 1971 and I had both road and track teams in 1972. Dave Lloyd's win in the William Tell Grand Prix was our first international win in 26 years. We got bronze medals in the team pursuit in the Munich Olympics in 1972 through Mick Bennett, Ian Hallam, Ron Keeble and Willi Moore. Phil Bayton and Phil Edwards were fifth and sixth in the road-race, won by Hennie Kuiper. Then we had silver medals in the world team pursuit in 1973 at San Sebastian. Now, that's a successful team.

But not as successful as the track team was later to become.

There was a moment during the Olympic Games of 2004 when the commentators on French television were waiting to see how their nation's favourite, Arnaud Tournant, would do in the kilometre. He was last but one to ride and after him came the British rider, Chris Hoy. Tournant was beaten by a sliver of a second and French television was forced to concede that the decade-long run of French superiority on the track was over.

But why, the commentators wanted to know, had it succumbed to a nation that had only erratically done well in cycling – any cycling – and yet now appeared to dominate on the track? Daniel Morelon, the silver-haired former World Sprint Champion who runs part of France's track training scheme, said it was because Britain had copied France's methods. In turn, France itself had borrowed ideas from the old East Germany. Asked for another reason, the more recent star of French sprinting, Florian Rousseau, said it was because Britain had many more good tracks than France. It was his way of campaigning for more government money for French cycling.

In fact, Britain has no more good tracks than does France. Two, in fact, France's being in Bordeaux – a white elephant of a stadium – and near the Mediterranean at Hyères, the latter without a roof. Rousseau perhaps assumed that absence of news from Harlow, Meadowbank and Leicester wasn't to be taken as a suggestion they'd all been pulled down.

Britain won four medals at the Athens Olympics of which two were gold: apart from Hoy's overturning of Tournant, there was gold for Bradley Wiggins in the Individual Pursuit; silver in the Team Pursuit; and bronze in the Madison. In the same year that David Millar's abrupt exit from professional cycling confirmed the country's strange inability to hold its own on the road, Britain became leading nation on the track. With no more tracks than France

– although in a country geographically smaller so that those tracks are closer to centres of population – Britain has displaced France as the world's best.

It has come about because British Cycling has placed most of its resources on the track. That is where the talent lies and where the successes come. It is the part of cycling that can be best improved by coaching and by sponsorship, especially government sponsorship. And since success breeds success, effort follows more effort. To do well on the road, on the other hand, means leaving the country and seeking a contract abroad. That contract secured, training and racing can barely be touched by coaches back in Britain.

Sponsorship to develop cycling is put into what is called a Performance Plan. Some say it concentrates too much, perhaps exclusively, on the track. And that, they say, is because the people who run British cycling have conceded that road-racing is in a lingering death. The police don't want it, and ask for more and more money and more and more conditions to allow it to happen. The fear of being sued after an accident involving someone not concerned with the race is so great that the officials who organise their races, in an hour or two each evening after work, are confronted by lengthy, time-consuming safety assessment forms. There is little to encourage anyone to organise a race on the road and no way for British riders to succeed internationally if they stay in Britain. Logic, then, says the money should go on the track.

But that's history repeating itself. The NCU demanded its clubs put their races and their money on the track a hundred years back. Then, too, they were worried about the police. And people who loved the sport pointed out what can be pointed out even more now, in an era when there are so few tracks: that those a long way from a track have no way to become track cyclists. For all that aspiring youngsters can watch Chris Hoy win medals for Britain on television, they can no more emulate him than a swimmer in Rugby can become world surfing champion. The facilities are just too far away.

Britain is the fifth largest nation in Europe, discounting the frozen areas of Scandinavia, and only a little bit different from Italy. Its population is one of the continent's largest. It has the fourth largest economy in the world. It had the first bike-race winner in the world. And yet on the road it ranks almost nowhere. Even Ireland has had more Tour winners than Britain, an arithmetically simple feat, admittedly, since Britain has had none. So why?

We keep coming back to Gerald O'Donovan and his worry that something about British riders means they don't do well off their island. Some have done brilliantly, but the fact that you can probably name them all makes the point. So why do people from an island within sight of France find it so difficult to be happy beyond Calais? Could it be that Britain is more 'abroad' than other countries? It seems odd to read that of your own country when to you it's everyone else who's a foreigner. But look at it from the other direction: France is England's nearest neighbour but England is only France's ninth nearest neighbour. France lists Belgium, Germany, Luxembourg, Switzerland, Italy, Spain, Monaco and Andorra ahead of Britain. More than that, all nine of those borders are on land. 'Abroad' for Frenchmen and for people in other Continental countries is a place they can walk to, ride a bike to, even somersault into. Those who live on the border know the other country and its way of life as well as their own.

In fact, most nationalities are little better at riding outside their country than are the British. Few Frenchmen ride for teams outside France, just as Dutchmen and Belgians (who share a language) generally ride only in each other's teams and Italy keeps its riders at home. Spanish riders, too, prefer to have their wages paid from south of the Pyrénées.

All that is understandable. But it's not a choice open to British riders. They don't speak the language of any European team. Some who went to ride for Raleigh in the 1970s said they were astonished, or at any rate at a disadvantage, when Peter Post spoke in Dutch. Dutch is not a difficult language – for all its apparent impenetrability, it shares common points with English – but the British have grown used to the idea that foreigners will speak to them in their own language. That's what happens on holiday. It comes as a shock to find there is a difference at work.

Bob Thom grew up in the era of circuit races at Brooklands and Donnington, then became one of the best road managers that Britain has ever had. Most of the great amateur victories of the 1960s, particularly in the Milk Race, were under his guidance. A few weeks before his death in 2004, he said: 'A major problem is in Britain being an island. The continentals cross each other's borders to race regularly and gain experience. In the 1950s and 60s we had strong riders capable of performing well on the Continent if they'd had the financial support they have these days. They went to the Continent, became discouraged or could not afford to live there and returned.'

To be a Continental professional in the 1950s and early 1960s was a determined business. It was a long way to go home, physically and mentally. Now, home is a motorway drive or a cheap flight away. That makes it easier to go abroad in the first place but, significantly, it makes it easier to come home again. That is one reason Australians suggest for why they, from the other side of the world, survive better than the British.

It doesn't surprise an Australian that the rest of the world is not like Australia. The British, used to 'Abroad' as a place laid on for their entertainment, may have a different view. In fact, there will be as many reasons as there are riders who buy their one-way ticket back to Britain. It's a depressing conclusion, but Britain appears to be mentally what it is geographically: close to Europe but not actually part of it.

So where does that leave us? Sadly, little better than we were after the war. In fact, if you go right back to the start of cycling, Britain is doing worse, on the road anyway. Then, British riders won Paris–Rouen and Bordeaux–Paris. It took until 1963 for that Bordeaux–Paris Classic win to be repeated, and that through Simpson.

There were world champions on the track every few years, from Norman Sheil in 1955 and 1958 through to Hugh Porter in 1968, 1970, 1972 and 1973 – no mean record. But Sheil was a working man and he had to get back to work the morning after winning. He says continental agents were 'amazed' that he didn't stay on for the revenge matches they could have lined up. When, having tried all else, he started the Tour de France in 1960 and then didn't finish, his career was effectively over.

Porter, like other British riders, felt too uncomfortable to stay abroad. 'He was like an exotic summer bird,' the Belgian journalist Jan Cornand once told me. 'He flew in, paraded his feathers and then, just as quickly, he was gone again. He could have made a great career on the boards as a six-day man, but he never did.' There have been others since, riders who establish what, to Continentals, is an impressive but puzzling reputation for winning world championships, but rarely being seen again on the Continent.

The same even goes for the trackies who have won world championships for Britain in more recent years. They are seen at track meetings but, considering they come from a country so close to the mainland, they are less well known on the Continent than Australian champions – because for an Australian it's too far to keep popping home.

The same applied when Chris Boardman became an international track rider and then a professional roadman in the 1990s. He was the member of a French team who spent as little time as he could in France, or indeed anywhere else abroad. His wife and four children stayed home near Liverpool and he flew back to see them. 'To succeed,' he said, 'you've got to make the sacrifices, live abroad and do the performances. I was the exception; I did it the other way round, did the performances and got my place in the team. Living at home was a bit of a compromise but if I'd gone the normal route and lived in France, I wouldn't have made the grade. I wasn't hard enough.'

From which you could almost draw the conclusion that if a man capable of riding the Tour and of taking the World Hour Record wasn't hard enough to succeed by staying abroad, more ordinary mortals must be just too soft. In other words British riders just don't have the guts. A disconcerting thought.

Could it be an inferiority complex, the assumption that riders from bigger cycling nations are simply better? Or discouragement, a feeling of having to swim against the tide? Mike Breckon is a former BBAR team winner who therefore has experience of 'establishment' racing in Britain. He has also worked with the Canadian national team and, on returning to Britain, with Raleigh's sponsorship of the time-triallist Ian Cammish and of a mountain bike team. The tale he tells of the difference between cycling – indeed of life – in Britain and North America is revealing. He says:

The scene is a Monday morning in an office in North America. They ask you if you've had a good weekend and you say that yes, thanks, you did.
  'What did you do?'
  'I went out on my bicycle for a ride.'
  'How far did you go?'
  'About 50 miles.'
  'Gee, that must have been great, I bet you feel good!'
  Now you have to imagine the same scene in a British office. The conversation goes exactly the same except for the last response. In Britain it's 'You must be bloody mad!'
  When I tell this story I always get a lot of laughs, everyone recognises how true it is. Why is that? Is it because British people don't like cycling, or don't like exercise, or *feel* that they shouldn't be seen to like it?
  So if the problem is a part of our culture, where does it come from? Has it to do with cycling specifically? Certainly you wouldn't get the 'must be mad' response if you said you had played football, though you might if you said you went running. I think there is a laziness inherent in the British character which induces a negative reaction to almost anything which requires violent exercise. If you look at the two top British sports, soccer and cricket, neither involves the need for endurance; they are mainly inborn skills.
  I have told the story for 30 years now of Barry Harvey. He was one of Benny Foster's boys, an East Midlands trackie who rode reasonably well but never won anything big. Then he emigrated to Canada and we met up there. Within six months he was back on his bike and sprint champion of Canada. A big fish in a small pool you might say, but Barry went on to ride for us at the Commonwealth Games in 1970 in Edinburgh where he won a silver on the tandem, took fifth in the kilo and provided some of the most entertaining sprinting of the games, going out to the eventual gold medallist, Gord Johnson. The

eight Canadian cyclists at the games took more medals between them than all 47 UK cycling competitors!

Barry was a different man from the one who grovelled round the tracks of the East Midlands. He was self-confident; he was determined; he was aggressive – indeed all the traits in his personality which had made him emigrate and go on from there. He is now a multimillionaire, living the high life in California.

How did that all come about? It was in my view, entirely cultural. He moved into a different world, was stimulated rather than put down, admired rather than sneered at, encouraged. The very basic stimuli of North American life turned him round, activating all the right things that were inside him but had not been stimulated before.

Maybe, too, there is something understated and orderly in the British character that produced that special attraction to time-trialling. That was a rebellious idea when it started, but it was a gentle rebellion, a riot not to cause offence, not to stand up for anything. It was so anxious not to be noticed that it conducted itself in secret, secret not only from outsiders but from the sport itself.

Time-trialling became the all-purpose sport, one which enthusiasts emphasised was not simply for the best but for even the lowliest rider, who could race against himself and his past performances, happy to improve his best by a handful of seconds even though the stars had beaten him by half an hour or more. At the same time, those stars were not to make too much of their success, and certainly they weren't to make too much out of it. Nobody was to be told where they were riding, and that same secrecy would guarantee that only cyclists themselves had any interest afterwards. Not for time-triallists any hope of national acclaim in a world where sports editors couldn't even be told a race was taking place.

To criticise time-trialling is to assume it is a less valid part of the sport. It is not. There is a wonderful ethic in competing anonymously for no greater reward than riding better than the week before. If that is the aim, then nothing beats it. But it is a dead end, not only because the years of secrecy were guaranteed to produce a shrill whistle of public indifference, but because the peak of British time-trialling is… British time-trialling. Nobody else does it. The most important championship is the British championship, because there are no others. The best in Britain is the best in the world. Flattering but nonsensical.

Bob Thom said: 'I am not anti time-trialling but I feel that so many talented riders remain testers [time-triallists] who could become excellent road-racers. Riders from a club ride time-trials, enjoy it and never ride road-races. Among them could be a potential top roadman.'

And as for making money from the sport… the same spirit that questioned whether George Mills had paid his fare to Bordeaux lived on for a century. Time-trial prizes were to be in kind and never in cash. And because a suspension from time-trialling for accepting cash anywhere else meant a ban from all cycling, the same was true of all British prizes. Riders were rewarded by canteens of cutlery, trophies and things they never wanted.

The trophies became a racket. Some were worth thousands even in the nineteenth century, especially in grass track racing, and the first to win one three times could keep it, put it on his mantelpiece or, more likely, sell it for its gold or silver. Time-trialling never had cups of that sort and it says something of the gentleness of the sport that even being repaid for expendable items such as tyres and handlebar tape was considered dubious.

At first riders were given vouchers to spend at a named bike shop, almost always the one which provided the voucher in the first place. When most riders were local, that was no problem. But with more riders able to travel to fast courses, a rider from Tyneside could be awarded a £3 voucher from a shop in east London. Enter the next stage, in which the rider could send the organiser a receipt for something he had bought and be refunded three one-pound notes by return.

It doesn't follow that riders will always go better when they are paid. But that was always the assumption. Why, otherwise, would the Olympic Games have been for so long restricted to amateurs? If professionals were no better, they could have been admitted from the start. On the other hand, there is a limit to how much time, travel and training a rider can do while having to keep a job. Riders like Arthur Metcalfe, who rode the Tour de France while holding an almost full-time factory job, or Les West, who worked throughout his time as a professional, don't prove that it's possible to do it; it's the others, who couldn't do it, who suggest what talent Britain subdued because it allowed riders no more than three quid a weekend.

On the Continent, meanwhile, things progressed differently. The word *amateur* is French. In French it means someone who loves doing something. It doesn't mean, as it does in English, someone who does it without being paid. The French, Belgians and Dutch never considered that to be the case. For almost all the history of cycling, they have taken the view that an amateur is someone who can win money, but isn't good enough to earn his living from it.

That was the distinction the British League of Racing Cyclists tried to cross by adopting independents. Merely having an independent class, a stepping stone to professionalism, acknowledged that professionalism was an ideal. It was hardly surprising that the greatest opposition came from the Road Time Trials Council, which never opposed professionals but saw its role as defending the amateur.

Fans of the BLRC – many still wear the lapel badge of a cyclist bursting out of a Union Jack – believe Britain's years in what they see as the wilderness of no road-racing cost the nation its place in world cycling. It is that, they say, that stopped the British being as interested in cycling as are the French, say, or the Italians.

Chas Messenger, one of the final officials of the BLRC and the manager of both Graham Webb and Beryl Burton in the world championship team of 1967, condemns other organisations' officials for refusing to make the sport richer and more attractive. 'During the years from 1900, nothing was done by the NCU to foster sponsorship or get together with the media, which was to their cost because others sports were embracing big businesses and the media and going from strength to strength. The cycling politicians of the day couldn't see beyond their noses.'

Britain has never established a permanent pro tour, nor a professional team that lasted more than a few seasons. British bike riders could win abroad but their reception in British papers was 'plucky Brit beats foreigners at their own game'. What the coverage emphasised wasn't the Britishness of the achievement, it was the foreignness of the sport. It was the coverage that French papers would give a Parisian knocking a six at Lords.

Nobody knows what would have happened if the BLRC had continued, or at least if that spirit had continued. It didn't continue because it was built on hot bubbles of protest and bubbles rub each other's sides until they burst. The BLRC burst. That was half a century ago. A lot has changed since then. Satellites, planes without propellors, colour television, pedals without toe clips, a prime minister in knickers. It's pushing it to say that the lost years of the first half of the twentieth century still take their toll on the twenty-first.

Britain isn't a land where new sports are instantly rejected. British TV showed as much cycling as it did American football and yet, at least for a few years, it was American football teams that were being formed and not new cycling clubs. Nor is it true that television creates sports. Far from it. It wrecked darts. And kabaddi, the ideal beach or gymnasium game (with the pleasing absurdity that competitors have to hold their breath, chanting 'kabaddi, kabaddi' until they burst), was shown for years on Channel 4 without making the slightest impact.

The truth is that some countries like some sports and others prefer different sports. There is pelota in Spain but none in Britain; Britain has cricket but a Frenchman couldn't even number the players in a team. The Dutch race across muddy fields on stilts; the British go in for Morris dancing.

Cycling was shown up even back in the days of Freddie Bidlake as a sport that Britain didn't really want. It didn't have the courage back then, for reasons we find hard to understand now, to stand up and say: 'Here we are, and here we stay.' It has conducted itself ever since in fear and paranoia, like a dog permanently expecting a fatal kick.

Bike racing in Britain has come a long way since James Moore and the Parc-de-St-Cloud. The shame is that Britain isn't interested. Bury St Edmunds, the town where the world's first cycling winner was born, has neither a plaque to his memory nor the bike on which he won. Nor does it want either. That's the state of public indifference after more than a century of trying. Sad, isn't it?

Appendix

THE TOURS OF BRITAIN

1945	Victory Marathon	am	Robert Batoot (France)
1946	Brighton-Glasgow	am-ind	Mike Peers (Manchester)
1947	Brighton-Glasgow	am-ind	George Kessock (Paris Cycles)
1948	Brighton-Glasgow	am-ind	Tom Saunders (Dayton)
1949	Brighton-Glasgow	am-ind	Geoff Clark (ITP)
1950	Brighton-Glasgow	am-ind	George Lander (Fréjus Cycles)
1951	Butlin Tour*	amateur	Stan Blair (England)
	Tour of Britain	am-ind	Ian Steel (Viking Cycles)
	Brighton-Glasgow	amateur	Ian Greenfield (Comet CC)
1952	Brighton-Glasgow	amateur	Bill Bellamy (Romford CC)
	Tour of Britain	am-pro	Ken Russell (Ellis-Briggs)
1953	Brighton-Newcastle	amateur	Frank Edwards (Norfolk)
	Tour of Britain	am-ind	Gordon Thomas (BSA Cycles)
1954	Tour of Britain	am-ind	Eugène Tambourlini (France)
	Circuit of Britain	amateur	Viv Bailes (Teesside)
1955	Circuit of Britain	amateur	Des Robinson (Yorkshire)
	Tour of Britain	am-ind	Tony Hewson (Sheffield)
1956	Circuit of Britain	amateur	Dick McNeill (North-east)
1957	....		
1958	Milk Race	am-ind	Richard Durlacher (Austria)
1959	Milk Race	am-ind	Bill Bradley (England)
1960	Milk Race	amateur	Bill Bradley (England)
1961	Milk Race	amateur	Bill Holmes (North)
1962	Milk Race	amateur	Eugen Pokorny (Poland)
1963	Milk Race	amateur	Pete Chisman (England)
1964	Milk Race	amateur	Arthur Metcalfe (England)
1965	Milk Race	amateur	Les West (Midlands)
1966	Milk Race	amateur	Josef Gawliczec (Poland)
1967	Milk Race	amateur	Les West (Britain)
1968	Milk Race	amateur	Gosta Pettersson (Sweden)
1969	Milk Race	amateur	Fedor Den Hertog (Holland)
1970	Milk Race	amateur	Jiri Manus (Czechoslovakia)
1971	Milk Race	amateur	Fedor Den Hertog (Holland)
1972	Milk Race	amateur	Hennie Kuiper (Holland)

seven-stage race between Butlin holiday camps

1973	Milk Race	amateur	Piet van Katwijk (Holland)
1974	Milk Race	amateur	Roy Schuiten (Holland)
1975	Milk Race	amateur	Bernt Johansson (Sweden)
1976	Milk Race	amateur	Bill Nickson (Britain)
1977	Milk Race	amateur	Said Gusseinov (USSR)
1978	Milk Race	amateur	Jan Brzezny (Poland)
1979	Milk Race	amateur	Yuri Kashirin (USSR)
1980	Milk Race	amateur	Ivan Mitchenko (USSR)
1981	Milk Race	amateur	Sergei Krivosheev (USSR)
1982	Milk Race	amateur	Yuri Kashirin (USSR)
1983	Milk Race	amateur	Matt Eaton (USA)
1984	Milk Race	amateur	Oleg Czougeda (USSR)
1985	Milk Race	pro-am	Eric van Lancker (Fangio)
1986	Milk Race	pro-am	Joey McLoughlin (ANC)
1987	Milk Race	pro-am	Malcolm Elliott (ANC)
1988	Milk Race	pro-am	Vasily Zhdanov (USSR)
1989	Milk Race	pro-am	Brian Walton (7-Eleven)
1990	Milk Race	pro-am	Shane Sutton (Banana)
1991	Milk Race	pro-am	Chris Walker (Banana)
1992	Milk Race	pro-am	Conor Henry (Ireland)
1993	Milk Race	pro-am	Chris Lillywhite (Banana)